BULTMANN,
RETROSPECT AND PROSPECT:

The Centenary Symposium at Wellesley

HARVARD THEOLOGICAL STUDIES

Number 35

BULTMANN, RETROSPECT AND PROSPECT:

The Centenary Symposium at Wellesley

Edited by Edward C. Hobbs

BULTMANN, RETROSPECT AND PROSPECT:

The Centenary Symposium at Wellesley

Edited by

Edward C. Hobbs

Fortress Press Philadelphia

Library of Congress Cataloging-in-Publication Data
Main entry under title:

Bultmann, retrospect and prospect.

(Harvard theological studies; 35)
1. Bultmann, Rudolf Karl, 1884–1976—Congresses.
2. Smith, Louise Pettibone, 1887–1981—Congresses.
I. Hobbs, Edward C. II. Title. III. Series.
BX4827.B78B76 1985 230'.092'4 85–47734
ISBN 0–8006–7075–2

1777H85 Printed in the United States of America 1–7075

IN PIAM MEMORIAM
RUDOLFI BULTMANNI
ILLUSTRISSIMI MAGISTRI
LITTERATI THEOLOGI AMICI
GRATISSIMO ANIMO
HUNC LIBRUM EDITOR
DEDICAVI

Contents

Acknowledgments

Only through the assistance of many was this volume brought to publication. Special thanks are herewith paid to the following:

Wellesley College, and in particular its Department of Religion, which welcomed and encouraged holding a Bultmann Centenary Symposium;

the Annette Finnigan Fund, which underwrote the Symposium, thus providing the indispensable financial support that made the Symposium possible;

Mrs. Margaret C. Lafferty, Director of Special Events at Wellesley College, who was unflagging in her labors in preparation, execution, and follow-up of the Symposium;

my colleagues on the Symposium Committee, Professors Roger Johnson and Robert Ratner of Wellesley College, who assumed much of the responsibility for planning and conducting the Symposium;

the speakers at the Symposium—Hans Jonas, James M. Robinson, Schubert Ogden, Helmut Koester, Antje Bultmann Lemke, and Paul Lehmann— whose addresses make up the bulk of this book, and whose generosity in time and labor guaranteed the significance of the event; as well as Lucetta Mowry and Harvey McArthur, whose memoirs of Louise Pettibone Smith added to our appreciation of the first "Englisher" and "travel agent" of Bultmann, and the four alumnae of Wellesley whose letters about Miss Smith flesh out our picture of her;

Dieter Georgi, whose supplementary essay remedies a gap in the Symposium's examination of Bultmann's work;

Harvard Theological Review and its editor Helmut Koester, whose immediate and enthusiastic support made publication feasible, and our publisher Fortress Press, the preeminent publisher of Biblical scholarship in this hemisphere;

Professors John Dillenberger (Graduate Theological Union, Emeritus), Ingrid Stadler (Wellesley College), and J. Christiaan Beker (Princeton Theological Seminary), who prepared and presented critiques of the addresses to the Symposium as a starting-point for our discussions;

Miss Aimée Furman, whose ear-to-computer labor in an emergency assisted in the decoding of one very difficult tape-recording;

and the more than fifty scholars who participated in the Symposium and its discussions, giving evidence that the centenary of Bultmann's birth was not the commemoration of an ending, but the celebration of a beginning.

The Editor

Edward C. Hobbs

The Bultmann Centenary Symposium at Wellesley

When Rudolf Bultmann visited America for the first time, his initial port of call as well as his "headquarters" (as he later reported in Marburg) was Wellesley College. There, on September 21, 1951, he was met by his old friend and frequent summer visitor, Professor Louise Pettibone Smith.

In commemoration of this event, and even more especially of the centenary of his birth on August 20, 1884 (in Wiefelstede, then of the Grand Duchy of Oldenburg), the Bultmann Centenary Symposium was convened at Wellesley over a three-day period in September of 1984. It was planned as an event both retrospective and prospective. Bultmann's place in his own time was of course a major concern of the Symposium; his relationship with theology and New Testament scholarship, and philosophy as well, was one dimension of the event. But his import for the future of theology and of New Testament research was likewise of serious concern in both planning and execution of the sessions. That this was not a memorial of Bultmann's death, but a genuine celebration of his birth and of his continuing significance for biblical and theological scholarship, became abundantly clear as the sessions progressed over the three days.

The speakers for the Symposium represented a wide range as well as a cross-section of Bultmann scholarship. One of his earliest students, the philosopher Hans Jonas, and one of his last, New Testament scholar Helmut Koester, were joined by two of America's leading scholars and writers on Bultmann, theologian Schubert Ogden and theologian/New Testament scholar James Robinson. They were joined by Bultmann's daughter, Antje Bultmann Lemke, who is her father's literary executor.

The Symposium was planned also as a commemoration of Louise Pettibone Smith, who played such a major role in introducing Bultmann to America, both in print and in person. A New England women's liberal arts college might seem an improbable location for Bultmann's American "Standquartier," and likewise for the American celebration of the centenary of his birth. But Louise Pettibone Smith was never deterred by improbabilities during her lifetime, and the improbable became an actuality. The Symposium therefore included memorial tributes to her by two of her colleagues, Lucetta Mowry and Harvey MacArthur, and a major address on her life and its meaning by Paul Lehmann, who began his career as a colleague of Louise.*

Over fifty scholars from the United States coast to coast, from Canada, and even from Germany, gathered for the three-day celebration. There were discussions subsequent to each major address, initiated by brief critiques; the critics were Ingrid Stadler (philosophy, of Wellesley College), John Dillenberger (historical theology, and theology and the arts, of Hartford Seminary Foundation and the Graduate Theological Union, emeritus), and J. Christiaan Beker (New Testament, of Princeton Theological Seminary). The discussions were lively, often exciting, and remarkably contemporary in their concerns. Somewhat to the surprise of everyone, it rapidly became obvious that this Symposium truly marked the beginning of a second century for Bultmann, rather than the commemoration of a bygone era.

It was our intention from the start to include a summary of the discussions in this volume. Failure of the recording equipment to produce anything remotely like a coherent transcription of the many voices made this impossible, despite several attempts by various listeners to follow the speakers on the tapes. Rather than reconstruct the discussions from memory, it seemed more honest to omit them entirely.

The offer of a remarkable essay by Dieter Georgi, on a major dimension of Bultmann's work not covered during the Symposium itself, New Testament theology, has helped make this volume a much more well-rounded presentation of the issues.

To Rudolf Bultmann: teacher, scholar, theologian, this volume is thankfully offered and dedicated.

*Louise Pettibone Smith was born on October 4, 1887 and died on January 2, 1981.

▶
The photograph is Professor and Mrs. Bultmann at Wellesley in 1951 (Lucetta Mowry at left).

Bultmann and the Past

Bultmann's Papers

Antje Bultmann Lemke

A Philosopher Remembers Bultmann

Hans Jonas

Bultmann and Time: Ecstasies of his Temporality

James M. Robinson

Antje Bultmann Lemke

Bultmann's Papers

On the evening of September 21, 1951, my father writes: "After a ride through the city we came to Wellesley College, a large and dignified women's college located on an unusual campus." This is the first reference to Wellesley College in my father's American travel diary. For both of my parents, this was the first trip to the United States. Following the description of the architecture and the comforts of the guest lodge, he comments on the lively exchange with Louise Pettibone Smith, her colleagues and her students. The report concludes: "I was also asked to speak in class on the influence of Moses on Paul and John. Here, I was especially impressed by the high standards of scholarship in this college."

From Wellesley they went, among other places, to Princeton Theological Seminary. Of this experience, he writes (in 1951, we must remember):

> I had to give my lecture on demythologizing. As a precaution, students were not invited, only faculty. The reason for this lies in the fact that the Seminary is supported by and completely dependent upon the Presbyterian Church. In contrast to all other schools and seminaries I visited, it appears to be very conservative. This was evident in the discussions and in the concluding words of President McKay, who emphasized the benefits the Church has, over the centuries, received from heretics. Indeed, he assured everybody that the most important impulses in theology have always come from heretics. Thus here, as in certain circles in Germany, I was considered a heretic.

The report concludes:

> We especially enjoyed seeing Professor Lehmann again, who had been a visiting professor in Marburg in 1950 and with whom I had many a glass of wine at the Sonne. Here, we again had

> enjoyable discussions, and he refreshed me with good wine at his home. But that had to remain a big secret, because Princeton Seminary is of course extra dry!

Diaries of trips are just one category of the Bultmann Papers. Before we review these together, I should mention that in his eighties, Rudolf Bultmann intended to destroy most of his papers. When his correspondence with Barth was published, he felt he had made some sort of compromise, and said, "This is the last time a letter of mine will ever be published." So on May 16, 1974, he wrote a note: "No letter, written at any time, to anybody, is ever to be published." The same applied to sermons. He felt that sermons and letters are directed to specific people, in a specific situation, at a specific time, and in contrast to manuscripts that are planned for publication, these are personal communications that should not be published. After some discussions with friends and family, he withdrew this threat and gave us the manuscripts of the sermons and several others with the comment, "I will leave the decision to you." Much later I found, in the early correspondence with Martin Heidegger, his pleas with Heidegger to publish some notes that were not intended for publication. In this 1924 letter, Bultmann writes:

> You must overcome your scruples concerning the publication of something that you do not consider perfect. Students who have difficulty reading your *Sein und Zeit* would benefit immensely if they could have not only your final result, but also could follow in the development of your thought.

And so, I thought this was a little justification of our pushing him a bit in consenting to (at least) not destroying these papers.

These papers include correspondence, manuscripts for his classes, and copies of class notes from his student years at Tübingen. I brought, just for the fun of some of you, the notebook which he kept from Heidegger's seminar, which is very systematically written with his own comments on them. There are plenty of notebooks from his student years and also from later times. In Tübingen, for example, there was Schlatter, in Berlin Harnack, in Marburg Heitmüller and Herrmann, among others. These are especially interesting for the study of some of these teachers. The papers also include manuscripts from single lectures, journals, newspaper articles, the sermons already mentioned, and scripts from radio and T.V. interviews. As did many people in his times, he used the blank, reverse sides of letters as writing paper. So sometimes the back is almost as interesting as, or more interesting than, the front of the sheet! Just the other day I found, on page 30 of his comments on Kamlah's *Christianity and Self-Assertion*, an invitation from Hermann Diem to give the lecture on "New Testament and Mythology" on September 8, 1940. There are many such dated events to fill in lacunae in the correspondence. These back sides of the manuscripts are not only very interesting but also entertaining because they also contain wine bills and cigar bills and things like that—his vices are very easily seen! Maybe that's why he wanted to destroy them! Among all these miscellaneous materials are also his poems. Some of you may know that Karl Barth thought that my father was a much better poet than theologian, and that he should have stayed with that!

Now, following my father's wishes, we do not plan to publish a series of volumes as is now done posthumously with many scholars, where everything that can be found is published. What we now plan to do is to publish occasional volumes according to known or anticipated interests. Two volumes have come out in August of this year: a volume of his sermons (*Das Verkündigte Wort*) edited by Erich Grässer, and the volume of the *Theological Encyclopedia* (*Theologische Enzyklopädie*) edited by Eberhard Jüngel and Klaus Müller. They had six (or five and one-half) versions of the Encyclopedia lectures my father had given between 1926 and 1936, and to combine them into one volume was a really monumental work. But this is the kind of publication that will come out of these papers. While the sermons are selections, they go from his students days (even before he finished his studies, when he substituted for his relatives who were ministers in Oldenburg) to his last sermons; thus this is a relatively complete collection. As to his other works, his dissertation has been published; his Habilitationsschrift (which has never been published before) and the "Entmythologisierung" (which was out of print) will be out in November; and a few other volumes are, so to speak, "in the making." We have formed a small committee: Eberhard Jüngel, Rudolf Smend of Göttingen, Bishop Eduard Lohse who is also a New Testament scholar, and myself, to plan what would be of interest, what could be published. And the next volumes will probably be a volume of correspondence with ministers, another with teaching theologians, one with philosophers, one with classical philologists. We thought that rather than have a chronological collection of letters, it would be nice to have them organized by the subjects; so, for example, classical philologists might be more interested in reading what is of special interest to them. One can always rearrange them into strict chronological order without too much difficulty.

Amazing in all the materials, especially the correspondence, is the continuity and the unity of Bultmann's life and thought, from his very first letters as a student at the Oldenburg Gymnasium, where he interprets the faith to some younger people, to the last ones, from the Calvinstrasse [his home address] in Marburg. Rather than reporting to you about the interesting aspects of the correspondence, I thought I would give you some examples.

At the outset of his theological studies at Tübingen in 1903, he writes to his parents about his intentions "to be at home in four other disciplines." Thus, he sets out to meet students in law, in medicine, in history, and in philosophy. He is successful. And in the next year (1904), when he leaves Tübingen, he exchanges letters with students in these disciplines.

Among the surviving correspondence, that with the medical student and future pathologist, Walther Fischer, is the most complete and perhaps the most interesting. They started corresponding in 1904, and continued until they died. After they each married, they corresponded more rarely, but from 1904 until 1918, it is very lively exchange. On August 8, 1904, he asked his friend in a letter from Berlin:

> Have you by chance seen a volume of the *Popular History of Religion*, a series that was founded recently? I would like to know who reads these publications since attempts of this kind are vital right now. Our church has been withholding much scholarship and criticism from lay people, and she has to act quickly or she will repent bitterly. Only education (*Bildung*) can overcome the current sad state of affairs. We can, of course, criticize much of current theological scholarship; Bousset's *Jesus*, for example, does not show Jesus with any depth. But hand in hand with lay people it will get much further than in its current isolation.

On New Year's Eve of the same year, he writes:

> The closer I get to my final exam, the greater are my doubts about our church, whose servant I will become. The old orthodoxy had a fine, firm structure, and was easily able to satisfy those in need of faith. The structure has collapsed and nothing new is there to take its place. What is passed off as new is, in my view, not able to withstand any storm. Have you read Bousset's *Jesus*? I'm afraid that if he cannot offer anything else about Jesus, the end of the Protestant Church is close.

And he continues on January 27, 1905:

> The Catholic Church knows how to satisfy its members; as Sohm stated in his *Church History*, every human being is, by nature, Catholic. The Protestant Church has failed in its mission a long time. You feel that the justification for the existence of the Protestant Church lies in its specific Christian ethics. I agree with you; however, I want to say something very different: the justification for the existence of Protestantism lies not in Christian ethics, but in Christian religion. The Church must give her members more than codes of ethics. I see the fulfillment of Christianity not in ethics, but in religion, in faith in God, in the concept of the kingdom of God. No moral system, alone, can satisfy; it only repeats "You must." For the true person, however, *Können*, *Müssen*, *Wollen*, "You can, you must, you want," must be one. The question, "How should I act?" will never do. We must ask, "What shall I do?" Whatever we want or pretend, the real motive of our action is the inner desire for happiness, or I would prefer to say, the feeling of my dignity as a person. You may ask, now, how I reconcile these views with my desire to belong to and to confess with the Christian Church. Well, in the following way. Christianity is *the* religion. It was that in its time, as we can see in the New Testament. This is the religion I want today, and I consider it unhistorical thinking if someone says what we have now is not Christianity any longer. Much has, of course, changed, but we do have the right to name ourselves after our originator, to see ourselves as an organic phase of development of a historic entity. And finally, we should not forget that two thousand years ago people lived to whom we are related. The differences centuries have brought are usually exaggerated. They are aspects of the individual human being that never change, that are today as they will be tomorrow. I might almost venture to say that nothing develops except the content of our conceptions, our ideas.

Here in 1904, in his second student year, he already articulates the questions which he tried to address throughout his life.

In a lighter vein, he writes in April 1905 from his home in Oldenburg, in response to his friend's internship in a country doctor's practice:

> I'm looking forward to the time when I have my own parish somewhere in the country. While I cannot cure the farmer's stomachs, I hope to get acquainted with them individually. In some ways, our tasks are related; and I think that in many ways the physician is able to get much closer to the people than the

> pastor. How good it would be if we could begin our careers together at some village near the North Sea.

Back in Berlin, he often writes about his courses in the University. In a letter of June 1905 we read:

> My main annoyance is currently dogmatics. We really do need a reform! What nonsense is taught about "Revelation," "Trinity," "Miracles," "Divine Attributes"—it is frightening! And everything is done out of love for tradition. I have sadly had ample opportunity to observe in my own home, how people can cling to their inherited customs and how much unhappiness results from this. When we don't see this with our own eyes, we cannot really comprehend it. Unless someone like Schleiermacher pushes all of theology a major step ahead, it will fall apart. However impressive the advances in historical research, the right spirit is missing—the spirit that would embrace all achievements of historical theology, that would utilize these achievements systematically, and thus create the basis for a new theology. Unfortunately, Harnack is not the man for this. He is too much of a scholar.

Interesting also is the exchange with the law students whom he had befriended in Tübingen and with whom he corresponded on the ethics of decision making in concrete situations. One of these friends wrote in 1906 to Marburg, where in the meantime my father finished his studies:

> How are you doing Rudi? What about the salvation of your soul? Are you pursuing this great path that leads to a village ministry, or is there any prospect of having a "Bultmann Case?" If Lahusen and I will be faithful and loyal *Consistorialräte* (church officials), we will handle this case with grace and without consideration of the person, yet with pleasure.

Now, the demythologizing issue certainly developed in a way into the "Bultmann Case," and I think it is amusing to see that these friends apparently detected something in the student that anticipated the future.

In the next year he concluded his studies in Marburg, then spent a year as a Latin teacher in Oldenburg. Next he was assistant to Professor Heitmüller in Marburg, and then became an associate professor in Breslau followed by Giessen. In 1921 he returned to Marburg where he remained until his death in 1976. Quite rightly, many people say his life was very uneventful. It really was. He stayed in Marburg all the time (aside from coming here!). In that respect he certainly was not like today's travelling theologians and philosophers.

The correspondence with his friends, from 1916 on a stream of letters to his future wife Helene Feldmann, and gradually the correspondence with his students and colleagues give us many clues for what he read and thought. I find the earlier letters especially interesting because they give us insight into the years that precede his own lectures and his publications. For almost forty years, from 1937 (the year I left home) until 1976, he wrote every Sunday (unless I was in Marburg, of course) a chronicle of the weekly events. This includes World War II and a semester in Zürich in 1953 where he met Martin Heidegger for the first time since the early 1930's. And some of these letters are really fascinating; he writes what he reads, he writes what he reviews, the plays they are reading, the poets, and so on, thus it is almost like a diary from 1937 to 1976.

Some of the occasional exchanges on specific issues—correspondence, for example, with Auerbach, Martin Buber, Albert Schweitzer—are quite interesting, precisely because they do deal with specific issues, even though they do not span many years. In later decades, the correspondence with ministers about their day-to-day problems, his critical but friendly exchange with Ernst Käsemann, Dorothee Sölle, and several of his former students, and the extensive responses to books of younger theologians, show an amazing range of concerns. The published correspondence with Karl Barth gives a good impression of the significance of some of this material not only for theological scholarship and for church history, but I think also for the cultural history of our century. It also shows how theologians who disagree fundamentally can maintain a fruitful exchange and can remain friends.

From the twenties to the forties one of his best friends was Hans von Soden, a theologian who came to Marburg a couple of years later than Bultmann. I would like to read to you from just one letter. In December 1923 Bultmann wrote:

> Concerning the number and motivation of students, we have had another fine winter. In my exegesis course, I am discussing Barth again. His *Epistle to the Romans* is certainly an amazing work, and though I find its exegesis artificial and allegorizing, I find its questions most fruitful for any effort of interpretation. My seminar confirms this; under the debatable title "The Ethics of Paul," I treat the position of the justified in the world. This seminar is especially instructive because our new philosopher, Heidegger, a

> student of Husserl, participates in it. He comes from Catholicism, but he is totally a Protestant. This he showed convincingly when, the other day, he spoke in a debate after a lecture by Hermelink on Luther and the Middle Ages. Not only is his knowledge of scholasticism excellent, but he knows Luther much better and caused some embarrassment because he had understood the issue on an equal level with Hermelink. I also noticed with interest that Heidegger is familiar with contemporary theology. He is especially an admirer of Herrmann, and knows Gogarten and Barth. You can imagine how important it is for me that you come here to join us in our debates. The older generation is unable to do this because they do not grasp the problems with which we are concerned. Of course I must add that this applies not only to the older generation, as an article on "Est Deus in nobis" by Bornhausen in the *Christliche Welt* demonstrates. This lack of comprehension became also evident at a recent debate of the issue of whether the Church should proclaim the Word of God or whether she should also become directly involved in social work. I took the position that the former was our task since social work cannot be done effectively without strong background in the field and without the well-founded program. Without either of them there would be quackery and playing with the symptoms. To establish contact from person to person, to build human bridges, is a human necessity; it cannot be called social work. I also emphasized that the proclamation of the word is the task, indeed the office, of the Church. This did not imply that we just preach on Sundays in big, empty city churches, but to preach at those places and in such a way that it can be heard. For that, it is absolutely necessary that the theologian know the social conditions of his community and society, and that he share the responsibility for these.

Every letter is like that: packed with what he is thinking about. I selected these excerpts for tonight because they are from the first letter in which Heidegger, who had just arrived in Marburg, is mentioned. It also deals with the issue of theology and society, with theology and politics, a subject that appears again and again in the Hitler years and, in the end, in the correspondence especially with Dorothee Sölle which I have already mentioned. I would like to add an excerpt from one of many Heidegger letters. As most of you know, Heidegger came to Marburg in 1923 and left in 1928 for Freiburg. From 1928 on they corresponded very regularly, but then it gradually petered out. Later on it was primarily through postcards, plus one or two letters. But from 1928 to 1932 there is a rather intensive correspondence. So in December 1932 he asked Heidegger whether he might dedicate a collection of essays to him. He wrote:

> The title will be: *Faith and Understanding* (*Glauben und Verstehen*) [i.e., vol. 1]. With this title, their commonality is expressed. In as far as some of the essays have a systematic character, the aim of the basic question is: "What kind of understanding is implied in faith?" Most of them also ask the exegetical, i.e., biblical/theological, question concerning the understanding of kerygma and faith in the New Testament. In recent years I have let my systematic studies rest, or have pursued them only so far as I needed them for the interpretation of the New Testament. For this reason I also did not take up the old question of the relationship between theology and philosophy.

Correspondence dealing with demythologizing extended to the last year of his life. And just as when he was a student and had written to his friend, in 1904, "Theology will come much further hand in hand with the laity than it will alone," he continued to answer questions from the laity. In August 1975, when he was 91, he replied to a Mr. Frazier, a physician in North Carolina, as follows:

> I have been asked what my personal faith in heaven and hell is. The traditional conception of heaven takes heaven to be a locality above the earth. I regard this conception as mythological. Nevertheless it has an existential meaning. Heaven means a reality beyond the reality of the earthly world. Heaven signifies the transcendent reality of which we can speak when we recognize that our personal existence cannot find its true self in its earthly worldly plight. When we become aware of this transcendent reality, we lose our anxiety about the future. We become independent of all ideologies that try to offer us blueprints of the future, although they are constantly changing. We also are free of the desire to subject others to our will. We accept them in their differences and can meet them with trust and love. We are also free from anxiety in the face of the tragedy of fate, because we see it as a step into the future—as hidden and incomprehensible as it may be at the moment. I believe, by the way, that the primitive conception of heaven as a physical locality is based on the sense that there is a transcendent reality; only it has not yet been transformed into a reasoned reflection. The same considerations apply to the conception of hell. Its existential meaning is not that of an image of a physical place below the world full of torments. Instead, it is the recognition of the power of evil, indeed, the evil of the poisoned and poisoning atmosphere which humankind has created for itself when we began to assume that we could create security through scientific knowledge and the ability to dominate

the earth. With this attitude, the world does become hell. Such confusion leads to a battle of all against all. Here are the roots of our doubts, our questioning of the meaning of life. This, then, can lead to resignation, to desperation, and as we see today, even to suicide. Our faith in the transcendent world cannot be a scientific theory, but is an attitude of our whole personality for which we must strive to do everything. Such faith will be challenged again and again by doubts and many temptations. We can only overcome these if we are open to the revelation of the truth and the strength and power of the transcendent reality. This revelation occurs again and again in our encounter with others who offer us trust and love in spite of our own shortcomings. Whoever openly receives such trust and such love will radiate trust and love to others. Whoever strives for this attitude will gain his freedom and faith ever anew.

Hans Jonas

A Philosopher Remembers Bultmann

This is not only the centenary year of Rudolf Bultmann, one hundred years since his birth; it is also the sixtieth anniversary of my first meeting him in Marburg in 1924. I did not go to Marburg to study with him. I had been drawn to Freiburg in 1921 to study philosophy with Edmund Husserl; but since the beginners were not admitted to his seminar immediately, we had the almost shaking experience of studying in a pro-seminar with a young Privatdozent who assisted Husserl, named Martin Heidegger. I was thus thrown without any choice into the circle of Heidegger students, who were at the same time profoundly bewildered and profoundly impressed, who felt that something extraordinary was going on. Speaking for myself, I understood very little, but felt, "This is it!" A whole young generation came under Heidegger's spell. He accepted a call to Marburg/Lahn in 1923, and his faithful students, including myself a year later, followed him.

One of the most wonderful combinations came about in Marburg, namely a close friendship between Heidegger and Bultmann. In Heidegger, Bultmann encountered in a certain way his philosophical destiny. Up to then, he must have been more or less under the spell, or at least in the general tradition, of academic neo-Kantian philosophy. I think Kantianism was perhaps closest to his way of thinking; and though he always had an interest in philosophy, I am not sure that he expected any great help from that quarter. In Heidegger, suddenly, he discovered something which could be put to use in interpreting the New Testament, the Christian message or kerygma: namely existential philosophy, the interpretation of human existence by an approach which generated its own concepts for penetrating the inmost concerns of human existence, and could be turned into tools of interpretation.

It was almost "bon ton" among certain of Heidegger's disciples to go also to Bultmann and study New Testament theology and, if admitted, to enter Bultmann's seminar on New Testament; and vice versa, for the better or more favored or serious students of Bultmann to go to Heidegger's lectures and, if admitted, also to be members of his seminars. As a result this consensus of young minds came about: study both fields! While I had continued the study of Old Testament for three semesters in Berlin during my early student years under Gressmann and Sellin in addition to attending the "Hochschule für die Wissenschaft des Judentums," I found myself, through this combination, though an "outsider," suddenly a student of New Testament theology.

Quite soon, I was an active member of Bultmann's New Testament seminar together with another Jewish student of Heidegger, to whom life-long friendship bound me ever after. She was Hannah Arendt, the political philosopher. We two were doubly "outsiders" to Bultmann's seminars: we were not only philosophers rather than New Testament students, but we were the only Jews in the seminar. Hannah Arendt was a very shy and withdrawn and at the same time a very passionate person. When she paid a visit to Bultmann to obtain admission into the seminar, and after he granted it, she suddenly said, in a rather threatening voice, "But I won't stand for any anti-semitic remarks!" Whereupon Bultmann answered, "Dear Miss Arendt, if any such thing should happen, I think the two of us together will be able to handle it!"

Here is something of the spirit of Bultmann: he completely understood, and at the same time, toned it down. Don't think that one cannot, with the right human attitude, cope with such a situation!

How did it come about that Bultmann inspired my dissertation, and my work on Gnosticism in relation to the thought of early Christianity and late antiquity, which almost became my destiny for several decades?

In his seminar on the Fourth Gospel, I accepted an assignment from Bultmann, namely to submit a report about the concept of *Gnosis Theou*, "knowing God—knowledge of God" in the Gospel of John. Bultmann's love was the Fourth Gospel, and through its medium came the point of contact with Gnosticism, especially with the newly discovered Mandaean documents. It was the possible bearing of the Mandaean nomenclature, of their vocabulary and their imagery on the problem of authorship and the whole meaning and spirit of the Gospel of John, which brought Bultmann into the realm of gnostic studies. The Gospel of John, which I actually liked least of all books of the

New Testament, became my destiny through this connection. When I accepted this assignment, I never dreamt of what it would lead to. For, when I prepared this seminar paper (in 1925 or 1926), I delved, of course, into the background which Bultmann himself had pointed out. I found myself in a world where I soon realized one thing: This is not just a task for a seminar paper. It kept growing under my hands. Well, the result was that I committed what in itself is an unforgivable sin. Instead of using my thirty minutes of the seminar session for the report and leaving the remaining hour-and-a-half for discussion, I kept talking from notes for two solid hours and at the end of the session still had not come remotely to the end of what I had to say. Looking back, I believe that this determined a good part of my future. Bultmann, very tolerant and very patient, spoke only a few words at the end, but later said to me, "Jonas, this was really important! You must go on with it! This is only a beginning." My answer was, "Professor Bultmann, I want to get a doctorate in philosophy, and not in New Testament." He said, "I will talk with Heidegger!" And so he did! He told Heidegger, my main teacher and under whom I was supposed to write my doctoral dissertation, about my performance, including its unfinished character. Heidegger broached the subject to me, and said, "If you want to, I am willing to accept a dissertation in philosophy on that topic, or on something connected with it. I have Bultmann's assurance that he will serve as a reader for that kind of dissertation." That settled it! (This is my only title to being classified here as belonging to the community of New Testament and Christian theologians!)

While I learned a lot from Bultmann about Christianity, and learned to understand the New Testament through him, it took me the better part of a lifetime to learn about him as a person. This was partly due to a difference of temperaments between this northern German from Oldenburg, where a restraint and natural taciturnity prevails, and my Jewish Mediterranean temperament, very much more verbose, much more explicit and expression-prone. In a curious way, we mutually enjoyed our diversity in this respect. He didn't lay his heart open; there was a curious mixture of profound recognition of our affection on the one hand, and on the other a certain distance, keeping the secret of one's inmost self and that of the other as secret.

When I came from time to time from America to Marburg in the years after the war, I always felt that some deep bond connected us; and without it ever being put into words, it was just because of that bond that the father-son relationship changed to that of friends, and from a certain time on he offered that we should call each other "friend," and henceforward we always opened our letters with "Lieber Freund." As the years went on, he showed a keenly sympathetic openness to the direction which my philosophical thinking took, and which as a whole moved farther and farther away from the area in which our community of subject-matter had originally consisted, namely, primitive Christianity, early church history, the interpretation of Paul, Augustine, and so on. When I struck out into very different fields of philosophical thought: philosophical biology, theory of organism, and later, technology and ethics, and critical history of the sciences (especially physics), he into his high old age was always not only interested to hear and to participate, but also to contribute. It turned out that to be a man of faith and devoted to the word of God was a very good precondition for being also a servant of the creative God, an admirer, an explorer, a learner about the created world in all its aspects. So that here, at least in this friendship, there slowly, progressively, without its ever being explicitly stated, grew up a kind of synthesis of theological and philosophical thought which did not merge their duality, but in which the give-and-take of two approaches to what is essential in existence and in being a human could be endlessly, fruitfully, never definitively, always partly disputatiously, but lovingly pursued.

James M. Robinson

Bultmann and Time: Ecstasies of his Temporality

The times of Bultmann were inauspicious. Though he received his education at the turn of the century, he was just beginning to establish himself in a career when the outbreak of World War I ended the stable society to which he was accustomed. It was no doubt due to his lameness that he did not himself serve in the war. But even so it was never again possible for him to pursue a normal academic career. The collapse of the German economy in 1918 extended by several years a hardship condition that was even worse than what Germany had experienced during the war. The resultant *ressentiment* over the conditions of the Versailles treaty led remorselessly to the regime of Hitler. That dictatorship led to World War II and the economic debacle that was only overcome with the currency reform in 1950, which came just a year before Bultmann's retirement. Thus there is every reason to explain why his career did not amount to much. But it did. So much, then, for economic causation in history. We turn to the history of ideas as its epiphenomenon.

I

The times were characterized in classical form by Friedrich Gogarten in 1920 as "between the times." His brief essay under that title was welcomed by Barth as a "dreadnought for us and against our opponents."[1] The striking title was elevated to the name of dialectical

[1] In a letter of 27 October 1920 from Karl Barth to Eduard Thurneysen, published by Thurneysen in "Die Anfänge: Karl Barths Theologie der Frühzeit," in *Antwort: Karl Barth zum siebzigsten Geburtstag am 10. Mai 1956* (Zollikon-Zürich: Evangelischer Verlag, 1956) 858. The translation here, and elsewhere in this paper, is my own. See *Revolutionary Theology in the Making: Barth—Thurneysen Correspondence, 1914–1925* (Richmond, Virginia: John Knox, 1964) 53.

theology's journal *Zwischen den Zeiten* (1922–1933). For this concept brought to expression their theological alienation from the 'Kulturprotestantismus' that had characterized the Bismarckian-Wilhelmian epoch just ended. The concept "between the times" involved only a vague premonition that the 'interim' would not be succeeded by the Messiah, but rather by the Antichrist of a Drittes Reich. Actually it was part of these theologians' profundity that they did not speculate about such matters, but focused on the interim itself. In 1920 Friedrich Gogarten characterized the times "between the times" as follows:[2]

> This is the fate of our generation, that we stand between the times. We never belonged to the time that today is coming to its end. Whether we will ever belong to the time that is to come? And if we, for our part, could belong to it, whether it will come so soon? . . .
>
> Have you not taught us to see in any and everything what man has made? Have you not yourselves sharpened our eyes for the human, by putting for us everything within history and development? We thank you that you did so. You created for us the tool, now only let us use it. We draw the conclusion: Everything that, one way or the other, is a human product not only arises, it also disappears again . . . Today is the hour of the sunset.
>
> We see the disintegration in everything. What that means is this: We have received the most acute feeling for what is human. We sense how today it has succeeded in permeating everything. Right into the most sublime thoughts of God. And in all seriousness we are moved by the thought as to whether today there are any people at all who can really think God. . . . We have all so deeply floundered into the human that in the process we lost God. Lost him. Yes, really lost—there is no thought left in us that reaches to him. They all do not reach beyond the human circle. Not a single one . . .
>
> The space has become free for asking about God. Finally. The times have fallen apart and now time stands still. A moment? An eternity? Must we not now be able to hear God's word? Must we not now be able to see his hand at his work?

[2] Friedrich Gogarten, "Zwischen den Zeiten," *Die Christliche Welt* 34 (1920) 374, 376–78; *Anfänge der dialektischen Theologie* (ed. Jürgen Moltmann; 2 vols.; Theologische Bücherei 17; Munich: Kaiser, 1962–63) 2. 95, 97, 98, 100, 101; "Between the Times," in James M. Robinson, ed., *The Beginnings of Dialectic Theology* (Richmond, Virginia: John Knox, 1968) 1. 277, 281, 282.

> Hence we cannot, may not, yet go from the one time to the other. No matter how much it draws us. The decision must first be made here. Before, we can do nothing with our whole heart. Until then we stand between the times. That is a terrible human plight. For all that is human breaks down and goes to ruin, all that was and all that is to be. But for that reason we can, if we only lay hold of the plight to the bitter end, ask after God . . . *We* have no time now. *We* stand between the times.

'Journals' as 'day-ly' documents do well to reflect one's concept of time. If *The Christian Century* represents the victors' incredibly naive and unrealistic view of the times, *Zwischen den Zeiten* did indeed bring into language that of the losers, which however is not to be dismissed as the pessimism of defeat, quite apart from the dialectic theologians' denials that their theology was primarily such an interpretation of the war. In retrospect even we should recognize that as slogans for the times "Between the Times" was more like realism, "The Christian Century" unrealism.

"Between the times" came later to be formulated as eschatological existence. For it was a striking hermeneutical translation of what, since Albert Schweitzer, was widely considered the essence of primitive Christianity, much to the embarrassment of theology prior to World War I: The dualistic aeons of Jewish apocalypticism, the "present evil aeon" to be followed by the "aeon to come," had with Jesus begun their 'dance of death.' The present evil aeon had been condemned (according to Jesus) "from the days of John the Baptist" (Matt 11:12) or (according to the New Testament) from Easter. The aeon to come was attested with forebodings, such as (according to Jesus) exorcisms (Q [cited according to Lucan numeration] 11:20), or (according to the kerygma and the New Testament) the resurrection. Its actual coming is imminent, though the coming has not actually taken place—the forebodings should not be taken for the thing itself. (One may recall the biting witticism of the time: Jesus predicted the kingdom but what we got was the church).

Already the Gospel of John sensed the profound substantive point given mythological expression in the language of the two-aeon myth, and thus the understanding of time was already to a degree dechronologized (i.e., demythologized) and elevated to a philosophical theology of sorts: "Now is the judgment of this world, now shall the ruler of this world be cast out" (John 12:31). "And this is the judgment, that the light has come into the world, and men loved darkness rather than light, because their deeds were evil" (John 3:19). Bultmann built his normative Johannine theology around this concept of world, in distinction from his orientation of Pauline theology around the concept of man.

Perhaps the power of Gnosticism over early Christianity and its fascination for Bultmann was that its myth in effect re-mythologized the substance of that apocalyptic primitive Christian myth much less chronologically, in a way more open to Neoplatonic philosophizing. Augustine's *civitas dei* launched the philosophy of history out of much the same mythological roots, in his case mediated in part through Manichaeism.

The discovery by Bultmann's Marburg colleague Martin Heidegger of the temporality of existence is a modern instance of such a transcending of chronological superficiality to get at the profundity lurking within that apocalyptic imagery of alternative epochs that determine humanity. In this sense Heidegger was for Bultmann what apocalypticism was for Jesus, Gnosticism for John and Manichaeism for Augustine: a preliminary understanding.

Albert Schweitzer's "thoroughgoing eschatology" had taken the mythological objectification for the substance itself, and hence ruled that the substance of primitive Christianity must itself be replaced by something having to do with reality (i.e., "reverence for life"). But this is a classic instance of what Hans Jonas has explained as the trick that the mind plays on itself, in taking its objectifications for what it is objectifying and thus getting distracted into relatively irrelevant and usually insoluble (and hence interminable) theological debates. When cut off from the tap root of its insight, the mind gets lost in the maze of its symbolic world, which, taken as literal, becomes the quite hopeless arena of theology.

The critical historical method in which Bultmann was trained had promised to peel off the layers of secondary accretion and lay bare the essence of Christianity, such as (according to Adolf von Harnack, the quintessential historian) the fatherhood of God, the brotherhood of man, and the infinite value of the human soul. But already Ernst Troeltsch had warned that the historian never gets outside of the relativity, ambiguity and inconclusiveness of the causal nexus of the all-too-human so as to be able to theologize about an essence. Harnack, after having written for the Kaiser his self-righteous declaration of war, seemed to have disqualified himself from serious consideration. Friedrich Nietzsche's co-religionist Franz Overbeck seemed to have the last word for the critical historical method: God is dead. Not that the critical historical method had killed it, for which it simply lacked the power. But the critical historical method was itself a by-product of the age of historicism, Cartesianism, secular humanism, which had in effect ruled God superfluous. The new Kafkaesque theologians took with radical seriousness this parentage of the method that had for a time seemed to elevate theology to a science, before shattering it to pieces.

II

A philosophical dimension of the Neo-Romanticism of the turn of the century was Neo-Friesianism, a revival by a Göttingen philosopher of a contemporary of and variant upon Schleiermacher, Jakob Friedrich Fries (1773–1843), who sought to maintain for religion its autonomy by tracing it back to its own *a priori*, which he called *Ahndung*, some kind of "intuition" for the holy:[3]

> He won over to his side the two Göttingen theologians Rudolf Otto and Wilhelm Bousset. Both wanted to give religion a firm foundation by grounding it ultimately not on history, but rather on a reality lying at the basis of all history: the rational ideas of absolute being, eternity, the absolutely necessary, the soul, and the deity—rational ideas hidden in the human spirit and demonstrable there by clarifying its nature. In these metaphysical ideas lies the *a priori* of religion. But these ideas, in themselves abstract, should work themselves out in ways that are perceptible in practical effectiveness in the form of concrete symbols in the history of religion. Bousset wanted to avoid the uncertainties of research on the historical Jesus by founding religion not on history, but rather on the *ratio*.

This is what is behind the book that may be, in its assessment of the history of primitive Christianity, the nearest precursor to Bultmann's own *Theology of the New Testament*, namely Bousset's *Kyrios Christos* of 1913:[4]

> It was first in this distinctive combination of the historical figure of Jesus with the proclamation of the congregation that the picture of Jesus was created which became so terribly effective, for

[3] Johannes Wendland, "Neufriesianismus," *Die Religion in Geschichte und Gegenwart*, 2d ed., 4 (1930) 499.

[4] Wilhelm Bousset, *Kyrios Christos* (2d ed.; Göttingen: Vandenhoeck & Ruprecht, 1921) 74–75. The second edition, posthumously edited by Gustav Krüger, acknowledges in his Preface, p. xv, the help of Rudolf Bultmann, who was also the New Testament editor in the series in which it appeared, Forschungen zur Religion und Literatur des Alten und Neuen Testaments 21, n.s. 4.

> the history of Christian piety. Only when the congregation placed behind the gospel of Jesus the figure of the heavenly Son of man, the Ruler and Judge of the world, and let his glory, half-hidden and concealed, shine through his history as if it were transparent, only when it painted the picture of the wandering preacher on the gold leaf of the miraculous, imbedded his life in the aura of fulfilled prophecy, and surrounded it with the excitement of half-unveiled mystery, only when it put him thus into a great divine salvation history and let him appear as its crown and completion, did it make this picture of Jesus of Nazareth effective. For the purely historical really never is able to have an effect, but only the living present symbol in which one's own religious conviction is presented transfigured.

In 1920 Bultmann's praise of Bousset was uninhibited:[5]

> Most of all Bousset's brilliant work *Kyrios Christos* (1913) permitted a completely new picture of history to emerge: the difference between Jesus and Paul is indeed to be seen similarly to the way Wrede had shown [in the either-or: Either Jesus or Paul].

One can put such uninhibited praise into perspective by comparing and contrasting it with a basically quite positive review of 1914 by another young liberal exegete, who however was not to make the move into dialectical theology as did Bultmann, but rather stayed within liberalism, Walter Bauer:[6]

> The loudest opposition will no doubt be called forth by the introductory chapters. With characteristic energy Bousset has cut the development of our religion on Hellenistic ground off from its Palestinian origins. Paul is separated from Jesus by the deepest cleft, and transplanted thereby into the closest proximity to Gnosticism. And even the veneration of Jesus as Lord does not connect primitive Christianity with the world of Hellenistic Christianity. I must concede that here I am not able to go along with Bousset. It seems to me that the result of the debate started by Wrede's *Paulus* calls for another judgment.

Bauer has anticipated much of the debate about form criticism and

[5] Rudolf Bultmann, "Ethische und mystische Religion im Urchristentum," *Die Christliche Welt* 34 (1920) 726; *Anfänge der dialektischen Theologie*, 2. 31; "Ethical and Mystical Religion in Primitive Christianity," *The Beginnings of Dialectic Theology*, 222.

[6] Walter Bauer, in a book review in *Deutsche Literaturzeitung*, 13 June 1914, col. 1493.

kerygmatic theology, although such tags are here anachronistic. The issue was still cast in the history-of-religions form of Bousset's position rather than the dialectic-theology form of Bultmann's subsequent position.

Lest it seem that such a development as is here being traced existed only in theory, one may interject the record of a comparable religious experience. On 26 February 1922 Karl Barth wrote Eduard Thurneysen and their friends a delightful (though so biased as to be really unkind) anecdote about the not-yet-Barthian "orator of the night and mystagogue" Bultmann, in which the religiosity of the history-of-religions school is as it were acted out in a cultic experience:[7]

> Sunday evening I went along to a "Michelchen" cult. Since after all as an outsider I could not protest, I was obliged for better or worse to sit there "silently praying" too, i.e. turned off, wholly without contact with the numinous. *Bultmann* presided over the hocus-pocus. Theme: Night. The night of sadness and of death, the mystical and the normal night, everything that has to do with night, darkness, sleep, rest, "quietness," twilight, bed, etc., was handled and considered in word, song and prayer on to exhaustion. To be sure the good Bultmann messed up the game, in that he took up half the time in a cult discourse, the conscientious consideration of how much for us modern people (in contrast to Paul Gerhardt) the night has lost the enchantment of the "awesome." Nonetheless: We were assured in a not wholly credible way that it is still a parable for us. The disciples of Emmaus with their fateful ". . . for it was toward *evening*" etc., had of course to appear more than once as crown witnesses, until finally nothing else remained but "in the name of God" to follow the call of the "tired limbs" ("you *long* for *bed*," *sung* with a terribly comic effect) and to blow out the candles of meditation that smouldered on the walls.

[7] In a circular letter of 26 February 1922 from Karl Barth to Eduard Thurneysen, published by Karl Barth, "Lebendige Vergangenheit: Briefwechsel Barth—Thurneysen aus den Jahren 1921–1925," in *Gottesdienst—Menschendienst: Eduard Thurneysen zum 70. Geburtstag am 10. Juli 1958* (Zollikon: Evangelischer Verlag, 1958) 28. *Revolutionary Theology in the Making*, 89–90. Bultmann's text, dated 18 February 1922, has now been published: "Nacht," in *Das verkündigte Wort: Predigten—Andachten—Ansprachen 1906–1941* (Tübingen: Mohr-Siebeck, 1984) 194–97. From the published text it is clear to what extent Barth's description is at least as much a commentary on where Barth was as it is representative of where Bultmann was.

Barth conceded that afterwards over wine at Martin Rade's house "Bultmann was much better than I had feared after his cultic effort."[8] In fact Bultmann was already rather far along toward becoming a dialectic theologian. But up to this time it had been largely under the influence of Friedrich Gogarten:[9]

> I agree very heartily with what Gogarten has said in his wonderful booklet *Religion weither* and still more deeply in his Eisenach lecture about such experience.

The first edition of Barth's *Romans* of 1919 seemed to Bultmann not really to solve the problems Barth himself was criticizing:[10]

> One has designated as Gnosticism the modern branch of piety that turns away from historical work. Rightly so, to the extent that this piety seeks to cut the connection with historical forces as a whole and reinterprets history completely into myth, as it seems to me indeed to be the case in Barth's *Romans*. . . . No matter how much I welcome the religious criticism of culture in Barth's *Romans*, just as little can I see, in the positive thing he has to offer, anything other than an arbitrary propping up of the Pauline myth of Christ. The judgment that Barth pronounces on "liberal theology" thus applies to himself to the same degree.

Hence in 1920 Bultmann still appealed to Gogarten (and in fact continued to be closest theologically to Gogarten):[11]

> Things are different in another strand that I see represented impressively in Gogarten: "Religion is so little to be conceived of without the experience of history that one can almost say of it that it is itself the experiencing of history (as we said, not the knowledge of history). In any case it is permeated through and through with the experience of history."

[8] Barth, "Lebendige Vergangenheit," 28; *Revolutionary Theology in the Making*, 90.

[9] Bultmann, "Ethische und mystische Religion im Urchristentum," 741 n. 7; *Anfänge der dialektischen Theologie*, 2. 45 n. 7; "Ethical and Mystical Religion in Primitive Christianity," 235 n. 8.

[10] Bultmann, "Ethische und mystische Religion im Urchristentum," 739, 740; *Anfänge der dialektischen Theologie*, 2. 40, 43; "Ethical and Mystical Religion in Primitive Christianity," 230, 232.

[11] Bultmann, "Ethische und mystische Religion im Urchristentum," 739; *Anfänge der dialektischen Theologie*, 2. 40; "Ethical and Mystical Religion in Primitive Christianity," 230. The quotation is given as from Friedrich Gogarten, *Religion weither*, 677.

By way of contrast to his rejection of the first edition of Barth's *Romans* as no better than Gnosticism, Bultmann had a basically quite positive approach to the second edition of Barth's *Romans*, no doubt due both to the evolution through which Bultmann was going, but also to the evolution evident in the completely rewritten text of *Romans*. On 26 March 1922, just a matter of weeks after the abortive Michelchen cult, Barth wrote Thurneysen a circular letter in which he reported on a letter he had received from a Swiss student studying in Marburg:[12]

> Bultmann has after all not only held his lecture on *Romans*, but during the last six hours of his course only occupied himself with that. He is giving "tremendous pains" to understand me. He sees that this does not go so rapidly, and has arranged lecture and course "more as a working group." "Instead of a critic we find rather an advocate." . . . Finally the negotiations went aground somehow in christology.

It may seem at first surprising that Bultmann understood the second edition of Barth's *Romans* as a philosophy of religion:[13]

> One may no doubt characterize Karl Barth's *Romans* with a statement whose formulation he would admittedly contest, but which, according to usage current until now, would after all be valid: The book seeks to show *the independence and absoluteness of religion*. It thus lines itself up—even though in the original form of a commentary—with works such as Schleiermacher's *Discourses on Religion* and Otto's *The Idea of the Holy*, with modern attempts to work out a religious *a priori*, and ultimately with Romans itself, which, in its radical opposition of works and faith, basically intends nothing other.

It is therefore ultimately not surprising that Bultmann analyzed the book systematically, not exegetically, but in spite of his basic enthusiasm also sensed the limitation of Barth's achievement:[14]

[12] Barth, "Lebendige Vergangenheit," 32; *Revolutionary Theology in the Making*, 94.

[13] Rudolf Bultmann, "Karl Barths 'Römerbrief' in zweiter Auflage," *Die christliche Welt* 36 (1922) 320; *Anfänge der dialektischen Theologie*, 1. 119; "Karl Barth's *Epistle to the Romans* in its Second Edition," *The Beginnings of Dialectic Theology*, 100.

[14] Bultmann, "Karl Barths 'Römerbrief' in zweiter Auflage," 370–71; *Anfänge der dialektischen Theologie*," 1. 138–40; "Karl Barth's *Epistle to the Romans* in its Second Edition," 117–18.

Thus even Jesus' resurrection is "no event of historical extension *beside* the other events of his life and death, but the 'unhistorical' relation of his *whole* historical life to its origin in God" (p. 195). "If hence the resurrection were to be in any sense itself a fact of history, then no reassurance, no matter how strong, and no reflection, no matter how subtle, would be able to prevent it too from appearing dragged into the see-saw of yes *and* no, life *and* death, God *and* humanity, which is characteristic of the historical plane" (p. 204).

Good! But does not this apply precisely also to the "Life of Jesus" in general? And what meaning at all does it then have to talk of the years 1–30 as time of revelation? Has not one then really turned completely away from the "historical Jesus"? "Jesus Christ is however the new person beyond the humanly-possible person, especially beyond the pious person. He is the transcending of *this* person in its totality. He is the person who has come from death to life. He is—non-I, my existential I, I who am in God, in the freedom of God" (p. 269). I can only understand all this in the sense that *the historical Jesus has become symbol*. . . .

I do not know if I understand Barth aright, but I can interpret his statements only as follows: Jesus is a symbol for the truth (preaching of the truth) that God's revelation is neither a psychic-historical fact or form, as such, so that one could read off directly the divine reality in methodically apprehended, "perceptible" history—for example at its "high points"; nor that it would be a fact immanent to all "perceptible" occurrence. So that hence the attempts of a certain kind of liberalism to have the revelation directly in the historical person of Jesus are just as false as all pantheistic talk of the revelation of the "God Nature" in the all. Hence symbol that God's revelation is always unhistorical and transhistorical, always unnatural and transnatural, always present only in a specific now in a specific person. Symbol for this is precisely the "Christ," and in fact not an idea (every rational approach is in fact eliminated), but as *verbum visibile*, as living present power.

How am I to get above and beyond this, I do not see, the more I make an effort to reflect in Barthian trains of thought about the meaning of faith and revelation. "Christ" is hence just as much a "sign" as, according to Barth, is baptism "in its paradoxical onceness" (p. 192), or as Adam is, in whom the imperceptible No of God becomes perceptible, where the historicity of Adam is explicitly declared by Barth to be irrelevant (p. 171).

That is to say, Bultmann has embraced dialectic theology's program of elevating real historical encounter, and existential decision based on it, to the *sine qua non* of Christian faith, but does not sense that Barth has actually achieved this goal.

By 1925 Bultmann was able to formulate more clearly his own criticism of the whole heritage of German idealism:[15]

> The attaching of the *existential* subject to history does not take place at all—at least if the existence of humanity lies not in the general, in reason, but rather in the individual element, in the concrete moments of here and now. Precisely for this reason the idealistic observer sees nothing in history which makes a claim on him, specifically in the sense that here something new would be said to him which he does not potentially already have, over which he does not already have control by means of his participation in general rationality. He finds nothing that encounters him as authority, he finds in history always only himself, in that the content of history is reduced to the movement of ideas for which the groundwork is laid in the reason of mankind. So he has control from the very beginning over all possibilities of historical occurrence.

Over against the idealistic heritage thus understood, Bultmann works out a theology of the word and a resultant exegetical method of criticism that is neither directed at historical factuality nor at some rationality to which the text is to be reduced, but rather to the subject matter peculiar to the given text, a subject matter to be taken in existential seriousness, in its call to be understood, and indeed to be encountered existentially, that is to say, as offering something available nowhere else in all of reality:[16]

> In all of these cases the word of the text is not able to speak in a genuine sense to the interpreter, since the interpreter, before one actually begins, and on principle, has available all the possibilities of what can be said, namely by means of the principle of one's approach. But without a doubt the original and genuine meaning of the word "word" is that it points to a subject matter lying

[15] Rudolf Bultmann, "Das Problem einer theologischen Exegese des Neuen Testaments," *Zwischen den Zeiten* 3 (1925) 337–38, *Anfänge der dialektischen Theologie*, 2. 51; "The Problem of a Theological Exegesis of the New Testament," *The Beginnings of Dialectic Theology*, 239.

[16] Bultmann, "Das Problem einer theologischen Exegese des Neuen Testaments," 339–40; *Anfänge der dialektischen Theologie*, 2. 53–54; "The Problem of a Theological Exegesis of the New Testament," 241.

> outside of the speaker, opens this up to the hearer, and thus seeks to become for the hearer an *event*. The possible rebuttal of an idealistic exegesis that it meets this requirement rests on the fact that it admittedly does not conceive of the speaking individual as a psychic subject or one determined by the history of the times, and hence can interpret one's statements as pointers to trans-subjective subject matters. But these subject matters are not those meant here, since they after all cannot become for the hearer an event. Rather, since their content is the system of reason, the nature of the rational spirit, they contain only what the interpreter disposes of as a rational subject even before one begins. Subject-matter exegesis hence seeks to take seriously the original and genuine meaning of the word "word."
>
> The character of this subject-matter exegesis is defined more exactly in that for it the possibility and necessity of a *subject-matter criticism* emerges, a criticism that distinguishes between what is said and what is meant and measures what is said by what is meant. . . . The subject-matter exegesis can find its norm only from the subject matter made available through the text, over which it did not have control in advance. The "taking of a position" that takes place in such subject-matter criticism hence has nothing to do with "value judgments," which would be made in retrospect upon the historical findings. Subject-matter exegesis hence stands in an oddly ambiguous or contradictory situation, since it comes to what is meant only through what is said, and yet measures what is said by what is meant. But this means that it never comes to universally valid statements as "results," but rather is always alive and in motion.

Such a statement makes clear that one has now arrived fully at dialectic theology, in language that has not yet bifurcated into a Barthian theology of the word and a Bultmannian kerygmatic theology.

III

The concept of myth as present in the Bible— first conceded to be present in the Old Testament, then the infancy narratives, then the public ministry and even Easter—is an unresolved legacy of the Nineteenth Century. For myths were classified as either historical or philosophical. If 'historical,' they were held to contain some element of historical occurrence. But it is quite indeterminate what if anything of historical factuality lurked in a myth. If 'philosophical,' myths contain some element of truth. But this tends to be bent in a rationalistic way into conformity to some ethical principle, some philosophy of religion, some rational idea. Exegesis had by and large resorted to one or the other of two policies: either critically to eliminate the mythical (separating the kernel from the husk), or to deny that it was really present at all. The latter alternative of denying its presence in the Bible tended to be rendered exceedingly difficult by the history-of-religions school, which removed biblical phrases from the modern contexts of church life in which they had been constantly updated and thereby kept alive and put them back into the contexts of Hellenistic religions where they had originally been alive, and where their mythological environment was inescapable. But the former alternative, eliminating the myths, came to be recognized as throwing the baby out with the bath, in that the mythical is the medium of meaning—the more kerygmatic, the more mythical. The movement back from Paul to Jesus in effect meant backing away from the cult of primitive Christianity that had made it a viable alternative among the mystery religions of the Roman empire. And the moralizing, pragmatizing modernization of the kingdom of God at the center of Jesus' sayings had been shown up by Albert Schweitzer's *The Quest of the Historical Jesus* to be an elimination of what Jesus had to say, motivated by one's frantic haste to eliminate his apocalyptic world.

It was the genius of Karl Barth to decode Pauline theology and reestablish it as the norm of Christianity. Yet he did so by means of genius rather than of method. Bultmann's review of the second edition of Barth's *Romans* had been an amazed positive summary of that core, with only peripheral concern with the lack of method. But in his review of Barth's *The Resurrection of the Dead* Bultmann came to grips with the methodological problem, in that Barth had yielded to the conservative 'out' of denying that the mythical was present, to which Bultmann replied in 1926: [17]

> It seems to me just as certain that in 1 Cor. 15 Paul is talking about such a history of the last things, as that he is actually not able to do so, and indeed does not really want to. That is to say, in the case of 1 Cor. 15 one cannot get by without thoroughgoing subject-matter criticism (not merely its occasional use, as is the case for Barth, after all, with regard to verse 29). For although

[17] Rudolf Bultmann's review of Karl Barth's *Die Auferstehung der Toten* (cited here according to the English translation by H. J. Stenning, *The Resurrection of the Dead* [New York: Revell, 1933]), *Theologische Blätter* 5 (1926) 1–14; *Glauben und Verstehen* (Tübingen: Mohr-Siebeck, 1933) 52; *Faith and Understanding*, vol. 1 (ed. Robert W. Funk; trans. Louise Pettibone Smith; New York and Evanston: Harper & Row, 1969) 80–81.

> Paul does not proclaim such a thing as an "ideology," yet there rests upon him as upon anyone else the necessity to say what he says in the terminology of his ideology. And it does not do simply to declare the ideological—in this case mythological—elements to be a "parable" or to get rid of them by making them mean what they do not mean! What Barth concedes for later Christian eschatologists, namely that they construct out of the biblical material a history of last things that actually is not at all ultimate, is true for Paul as well, who derives his material from Jewish or Jewish-gnostic apocalypticism. Paul too "stopped half-way" (p. 105). The fact that we as critics will perhaps get no further than did he, does not free us from the duty of criticism.

Thus Bultmann introduced *Sachkritik*, here translated somewhat pedantically, but it is to be hoped all the more clearly, as subject-matter criticism, the criticism of each statement as to its conformity of the central theme or subject matter of the text, rather than the apologetic effort to make every statement say what it should have said to conform to that theme. But Bultmann also recognized the critical necessity to penetrate through the mythically saturated text to find precisely what the core of the message is, before one can measure each statement by that core of meaning:[18]

> As much as I admire Barth's sure touch in laying hold of central ideas in the text—I could not proceed his way. For what we have to do with is not a simple side-by-side relationship between statements in the text that come from the history-of-religions religious background and such that are genuinely Pauline. Rather [we have to do with] interpretation and mingling. I think it would take a much more concentrated exegetical effort and terminological analysis to arrive at justified results. But even then—and such efforts of course also lie behind the printed expositions by Barth—I think one would have to emphasize much more the *risk* involved in such exegesis. It is after all no little matter to interpret away, so to speak, precisely those thoughts of Paul that at first are the clearest, and that were certainly important to him, e.g. the whole "history of the last things," be it by twisting the meaning of the text, be it by making distinctions critically!

It was Bultmann's and Heidegger's pupil Hans Jonas who, in his 1928 dissertation, stated philosophically the presupposition of the

[18] Bultmann's review of *The Resurrection of the Dead*, *Glauben und Verstehen I*, 57; *Faith and Understanding*, 1. 86.

method for interpreting the mythical in Paul that Bultmann had been working out:[19]

> In the metaphysical emanation and deprivation schema [of philosophical Gnosis] we come upon gnostic myth again in depersonalized, logicized form, i.e. in one regard indeed demythed (*entmythisiert*), and yet, because of its nature as hypostasized, still mythical. . . . We are also concerned primarily . . . to show how the existential basic principle we have postulated, the "gnostic" principle, if it really is capable of being disengaged from the mythological world of symbol and of being postulated as a more general principle, is here in a quite distinctive way drawn back out of the outward mythical objectification and transposed into inner concepts of *Dasein* and into ethical practice, i.e. it appears so to speak "resubjectivized."

Two years later (1930) Jonas imbedded in the nature of man this method for distinguishing the mythical from its meaning:[20]

> All this derives from an inescapable fundamental structure of the spirit as such. The fact that it interprets itself in objective formulae and symbols, that it is "symbolistic," is of the very essence of the spirit—and the most dangerous thing about the spirit as well. In order to come to itself, it by its very nature enters in upon this detour via the symbol, in whose enticing jungle of problems it tends to lose itself, far from the origin preserved symbolically therein and taking absolutely what is only a substitute. Only by means of a long process of back-tracking, after an exhaustive traversal of that detour, is a demythologized (*entmythologisiert*) consciousness able to approach the original phenomena hidden in this camouflage also in a conceptually direct way (cf. the long road of the dogma of original sin up to Kierkegaard!).

Here demythologizing as a term and as a method emerged eleven years before Bultmann's speech proposing demythologization was delivered.

Four years after his review of Barth's *The Resurrection of the Dead*, in the same year as Jonas' statement, Bultmann was able to discuss, much more conceptually than he had then, his distinction between the myth-

[19] Hans Jonas, *Der Begriff der Gnosis*, Marburg dissertation, 1928, 5–6, of which a copy is at Harvard University. It was reprinted as the Introduction to *Gnosis und spätantiker Geist*, 2. 1 (Göttingen: Vandenhoeck & Ruprecht, 1954) 3–4.

[20] Hans Jonas, *Augustin und das paulinische Freiheitsproblem* (FRLANT 44; Göttingen: Vandenhoeck & Ruprecht, 1930) 68.

ical and the point being scored, thanks to the vocabulary of Martin Heidegger:[21]

> When [a person] understands oneself in terms of what is transitory and temporary, one's being is not authentic being, but rather a being that has fallen prey to transitoriness. In the mythological way of conceptualization current in his time, Paul sees such *Dasein* as enslaved under spiritual powers, Satan and his hosts. . . . How little these mythological conceptualizations are speculative in character, i.e. how little Paul is trying to "explain" something with them, how much they are merely giving expression to a certain understanding of existence, is apparent from the fact that Paul, e.g. does not trace sin back to Satan (Rom 5:12ff.; 7:7ff.). . . . The extent to which Paul conceived of it at the same time in mythological thoughts is of secondary importance, once one sees which comprehension of existence expresses itself in them.

Thus more than a decade before the theological rigidifying taking place in the Confessing Church led Bultmann to propose the program of "demythologizing," the basic method had been grounded philosophically. The relation between *Sachkritik* and demythologization, and their distinction from the simple procedure of elimination characteristic of Protestant liberalism, was now clear:[22]

> If one may say schematically that in the epoch of critical research the mythology of the New Testament was simply *eliminated* by criticism, one could, to put it equally schematically, say that the

[21] *Die Religion in Geschichte und Gegenwart*, 2d ed., 4 (1930) 1032–33.

[22] Rudolf Bultmann, "Neues Testament und Mythologie: Das Problem der Entmythologisierung der neutestamentlichen Verkündigung," *Offenbarung und Heilsgeschehen*, Beiträge zur *Evangelische Theologie* 7 (1941); ed. Hans-Werner Bartsch, *Kerygma und Mythos*, 1 (1948) 25, 3d ed., (1954), 24; English translation by Reginald H. Fuller, "New Testament and Mythology: The Mythological Element in the Message of the New Testament and the Problem of its Reinterpretation," *Kerygma and Myth: A Theological Debate* (New York: Harper and Brothers, 1953), Harper Torchbook ed. (1961), 12; English translation by Schubert M. Ogden, *New Testament and Mythology and Other Basic Writings* (Philadelphia: Fortress, 1984) 12. In the 1948 edition, p. 25, the concluding phrase read "relationship of existence" instead of "understanding of existence." This may be a typographical error (*Verhältnis* for *Verständnis*). Yet compare Jonas, *Der Begriff der Gnosis*, 11; *Gnosis und spätantiker Geist*, 2. 1. 9–10: "The basic thing, that which makes a given concretion of *Dasein* specific, consists in its *relation* to the world—to its world—and to itself. . . . Every concretion of *Dasein* is such a relationship, 'is' this relationship. . . . The relationship takes places as an *understanding* of being." In this context Jonas spoke of man's "world-and-self-relationship."

> task today is to *interpret* critically the mythology of the New Testament. Of course the claim should not be advanced that there could not be mythologoumena calling for critical elimination. But in that case the criterion would have to be derived not from modern ideology, but rather from the New Testament's own understanding of existence.

Bultmann here refers to the "important remarks on the hermeneutical structure of dogma in Hans Jonas" "for the critical interpretation of myth," namely to precisely the passage from Jonas just quoted.[23] Already in 1934 Bultmann had drawn attention to the method Jonas had provided:[24]

> The method of the author [Jonas] of laying hold of the real meaning of a historical phenomenon by means of the principle of an analysis of existence, seems to me to have proven brilliantly its fruitfulness. I am certain that this work will fructify research in the history of ideas in many regards, and not least of all the interpretation of the New Testament.

The direction in which this relevance for New Testament scholarship would take in the case of Bultmann he indicated in a survey of 1936:[25]

> Only rather recently have we learned to speak of Gnosticism as a phenomenon in the intellectual history of late antiquity in general. In *Kyrios Christos* Bousset had not yet clearly recognized the independent significance of the specifically gnostic movement as the presupposition of Hellenistic Christian theology, especially Pauline theology. "Hellenistic mystery religions" and "Hellenistic mysticism" were the dominant concepts. Lietzmann in the first volume of his *History of the Early Church* showed that Gnosticism did not arise first on the basis of Christianity, as its "acute Hellenization" (so Harnack), but was rather a general phenomenon of the Hellenistic period. Yet he tries to understand it as a phenomenon syncretistic in its essence. Over against that view the (unfortunately still uncompleted) work of Hans Jonas shows that in Gnosticism there is developed a structurally unified and complete understanding of *Dasein*, new over against both the

[23] Bultmann, *Kerygma und Mythos*, 1st ed. 1. 25, n. 1; 3d ed. 1. 28; *Kerygma and Myth*, trans. Fuller, 16; trans. Ogden, 42, n. 6.

[24] Rudolf Bultmann, in the Preface, p. vii, to Hans Jonas, *Gnosis und spätantiker Geist*, vol. 1: *Die mythologische Gnosis* (FRLANT 51; Göttingen: Vandenhoeck & Ruprecht, 1934).

[25] Rudolf Bultmann, *Theologische Rundschau*, n.s. 1 (1936) 18–19.

> Old Testament and Greece, and of vast significance not only for Christianity with regard to its understanding of the world and its terminology, but also for the final development of Greek philosophy, Neoplatonism, and, mediated through both, for Western medieval history in general.

Just as the Neo-Friesianism of the history-of-religions school imbedded in Bousset's *Kyrios Christos* had produced the outline of primitive Christianity with which Bultmann began, just so the Heideggerianism imbedded in Jonas' *Gnosis und spätantiker Geist* produced the revision of Bousset's outline of primitive Christianity that Bultmann himself carried out in his kerygmatic theology.

It has not been our purpose here to summarize Bultmann's own theological developments, which would be a monumental task in its own right, but only to sketch some of the dimensions of his time as he encountered them and made of them participants in his own temporality. This is in effect the historicity of his existence.

Bultmann and the Future

Rudolf Bultmann and the Future of Revisionary Christology

Schubert M. Ogden

Early Christianity from the Perspective of the History of Religions

Helmut Koester

Bultmann's *Theology of the New Testament* Revisited

Dieter Georgi

Schubert M. Ogden

Rudolf Bultmann and the Future of Revisionary Christology

I

For some time now there has been little question about the most disputed aspect of Rudolf Bultmann's contribution to the ongoing task of revisionary christology. Beginning with a famous lecture by Ernst Käsemann in 1953, even Bultmann's own students who otherwise largely shared his theological position proved to have reservations about it at a critical point.[1] They had become convinced that, in criticizing the attempts of an earlier revisionary christology to support its claims by appealing to the historical Jesus, Bultmann had assumed the extreme contrary position of supporting his christology by appealing simply to the Christian kerygma. Consequently, they were concerned to show that, despite his strictures against such a procedure, an appeal back behind the kerygma to Jesus himself is not only historically possible but also theologically necessary. Subsequent developments have tended on the whole only to consolidate this position of "post-Bultmannian" theology with its call for a "new quest of the historical Jesus."[2] This is no doubt most obvious in the various political and liberation theologies, where criticism of Bultmann's theology in general invariably includes an appeal against him to the historical Jesus as the norm of christology. But from one end of the theological spectrum to the other, and across wide differences of confession as well as of culture and language, it has long since been agreed that Bultmann's attempt to make the kerygma the norm of christology now belongs to the past of revisionary christology rather than to its future.

It is not surprising, then, that the most recent revisionary proposals typically include considerable negative criticism of Bultmann's

[1] Käsemann, "Das Problem des historischen Jesus," *ZThK* 51 (1954) 125–53.
[2] James M. Robinson, *A New Quest of the Historical Jesus* (London: SCM, 1959).

contribution. Even in the case of proposals whose authors in other respects are expressly appreciative of his work and show every sign of being deeply indebted to it one finds continued objections to his position on the question of the norm of christology. In fact, the whole purpose of such proposals is to try to secure their own position on this question by representing it as the only tenable alternative to his untenable position to the contrary.

If one looks at these proposals more closely, however, it is by no means obvious that they give promise of a future for revisionary christology. On the contrary, the position for which they argue is in all essentials the very position of the earlier revisionary christology that Bultmann sought to overcome; and my judgment is that the difficulties involved in arguing for this position today are sufficiently serious that one has every reason to leave it behind. It is also my judgment that the criticisms of Bultmann that are usually made by way of trying to secure this position as often as not misunderstand his intentions in taking up his very different position on the question. Even if one allows, as I certainly would, that he may not have always expressed his intentions as adequately as he might have and that there may be ways of refining and developing his position that we today at least ought to consider, still the evidence is clear that the position he intended to hold is about as different from the one he is criticized for holding as it is from that of his critics.

But if these judgments of mine should prove to be sound, the question of Bultmann and the future of revisionary christology would need to be reconsidered. Far from holding the extreme contrary position that he is widely represented as holding, he would turn out to have opened up a third possibility distinct at once from two equally extreme alternatives: on the one hand, the position of an earlier revisionary christology as well as of his recent critics; and on the other hand, the position of perhaps a small minority of his followers, which these same critics mistakenly attribute to him. In that event, one could hardly avoid asking whether it is not the third possibility opened up by Bultmann's own position that most deserves further attention. As something like the common contradictory of both of the extreme contraries that should indeed be left to the past, it might well be the neglected alternative that opens out to the future.

The strategy of the following argument, then, is this: to compel reconsideration of Bultmann's contribution to revisionary christology by establishing the soundness of my two judgments. To this end, I shall discuss in some detail one of the proposals I especially have in mind in speaking of the most recent proposals in revisionary christology. Since my criticisms of this proposal will be largely negative with respect both to its own constructive position and to its criticisms of Bultmann's I want to stress at the outset that I nonetheless value it for its contribution to our common task. Its existentialist interpretation of Christian faith seems to me unusually clear and forceful, and any number of its discussions of particular questions have helped me to achieve greater clarity about my own theological intentions. This is not least the case at the very point of my greatest differences with it, fully confirming the truth that we are indebted to all from whom we learn—those with whom we are led to disagree as surely as those who elicit our agreement.

II

The proposal to which I refer is that of James P. Mackey, in his book *Jesus, the Man and the Myth: A Contemporary Christology.*[3] Trained in both historical theology and philosophy of religion, Mackey approaches the problem of christology as a systematic theologian. Thus his leading question, to which the book as a whole develops his answer, is the one indicated by its title: Why this myth of this man? If Mackey understands this question to ask for a historical explanation and structures the main body of his book accordingly, he also takes it to ask for a systematic justification, in the sense of what he calls a "living logic of faith" (253; cf. 173–74). "What is the logic," he asks, "which connects the developing myth about the man, Jesus, to Jesus' own myth? What is the logic which binds increasing faith in Jesus to the faith which Jesus' own myth embodied? This is *the* christological question, this is the question concerning the very origin of christology as such . . . " (184).

Mackey's answer is that the logic in question is indeed a logic of faith, in that it is the logic that connects Jesus' own faith in the Fatherhood of God and in God's coming reign with the faith he inspired in others by virtue of his faith. In places, to be sure, Mackey uses the phrase "the faith of Jesus" to mean "the faith which Jesus recommended," or which was embodied in his myth of the reign of God, as distinct from "his own personal faith" (296, n. 50; cf. 96, 163). But he is also explicit in claiming that the faith of Jesus to which any systematic justification of christology must finally appeal is "the personal faith of Jesus himself (the faith which was a quality of Jesus as

[3] New York: Paulist, 1979. Subsequent references are made parenthetically in the text.

personal subject, not the faith of which Jesus is object)" (163). By Mackey's account, then, the whole development of christology from "the earliest comprehensive myth" of the resurrection to "the full-grown myth" of the Nicene definition is justified as well as explained by Jesus' own personal faith.

> Jesus, because of the life he lived and enabled others to live, because of the grace he knew and allowed others to know, because of the faith he had and inspired others to have, because of the spirit he breathed into a dying world, in his verbal myth, his prayer, his table-fellowship, his practical ministry . . . Jesus, because of all this, proved significant, to put the matter mildly, in humanity's struggle for life over death; and people who prove significant in this way are the material of which myths are made, for which myths are needed. (189–90)

> It is the faith of Jesus which is still determinative of how we acknowledge him. It is that distinctive faith of his which, when we catch it from him, allows us to come in contact with the God he called Father, and which then demands that we acknowledge his role between us and God in all the ways in which the orthodox tradition did this. (247)

With this understanding of how even a contemporary christology must justify its claims, Mackey naturally argues for the theological necessity of a quest of the historical Jesus. "The distinctive faith of Jesus, the distinctive spirit of Jesus, is history. . . . If, then, as would-be followers of Jesus, we would seek the presence of the living God, we are directed, without alternative, to the human history in which it is both hidden and revealed" (262; cf. 3). But if a quest of Jesus is theologically necessary, it is also historically possible. As a matter of fact, Mackey argues that the quest of the historical Jesus "has never finally proved either to be misconceived in its nature or to have failed in its results" (248).

He recognizes, to be sure, that there is no possibility, given the nature of our sources, of reconstructing anything like a full account of the life of Jesus from infancy to death. "In fact, before what is known as his public ministry, . . . little or nothing can be said with historical certainty about Jesus of Nazareth" (122). Furthermore, "even of the few public years, not many purely factual data can be discovered," and "of [Jesus'] more particular deeds and words . . . it is difficult now to be certain of the authenticity, much less the more specific occasions of time and place and other circumstances" (123). But while Mackey thus allows that the old quest of the historical Jesus is indeed impossible, he nevertheless insists that "the faith of Jesus, radical as it is, is not outside the human historian's range" (279). Provided one agrees that "the only life of the historical Jesus worth recovering is the life that he literally poured into his public mission of inaugurating the kingdom of God," the fact that his public ministry is all of his personal life that his followers cared to remember and record is no problem (175). What they provided is "more than enough" for us to recover "the cause for which he lived and died," and thus to experience his own personal faith (123; cf. 50). Nor is the fact that all our sources are faith documents intended primarily to arouse the same faith in others any obstacle to such recovery. For "if Jesus' very life was an attempt to inspire faith of a particular kind in others, then, quite clearly, provided they got right the particular kind of faith he tried to inspire, no documents could be truer to his memory than faith documents" (122).

As for the present disenchantment with the quest, Mackey believes that much of it is due, "not to the kind of inadequacies which a professional historian might find in the source of material—for in this case . . . the source material is adequate to our purpose; the disenchantment is due, rather, to the persistence of questers in bringing to this material their own varying expectations and each seeing a different expectation fulfilled" (12). But if this suffices to explain the past difficulties of the quest, one may be guardedly optimistic about its future prospects. "The problem is not, as some think, that the quest has gone on too long or gone too far; the problem is that it has not yet been pursued with that combination of unqualified enthusiasm and unprejudiced professionalism which it deserves" (256).

Throughout this argument for the quest of the historical Jesus, Mackey is keenly aware of the alternative position of Bultmann. And yet, unlike many English-speaking theologians, he rightly recognizes that Bultmann's most serious challenge to his argument is not directed against the historical possibility of the quest. Bultmann is indeed "both heir and defiant defender of a long century of growing scepticism about the ability of the New Testament text to tell us anything at all certain about the historical Jesus" (164). But "we are not entitled to conclude that he is totally sceptical about the prospect of discovering the historical Jesus. His particular challenge to the historical quest . . . is based on considerations concerning Christian faith, not on distrust of the historical sources" (252; cf. 250, 255).

To be exact, Bultmann challenges the quest at the very point where Mackey speaks of "the logic by which the myth about Jesus developed from Jesus' own myth of the reign of God" (253). Just where Mackey tries to see "the connections of a living logic of faith, . . . Bultmann insists on an unbridgeable gap" (253). "The fact that Jesus is our Lord precisely because he, the historical Jesus, inserts into our history the challenge and the possibility of new faith and new life, by his preaching which is continued in various forms, by the prayer he introduces to our lives, by the ritual he invites us still to celebrate and the service to which he inspires us—this Bultmann is not prepared to admit" (253). On the contrary, "in Bultmann's system the specific content of the Christian faith, . . . the lesson we learn from the cross, comes to us from the risen Lord presented in the preaching and not from the historical Jesus. The man in whose action God acts, in whose destiny God is at work, in whose word God speaks, is the Son of God, not the historical Jesus" (252). Moreover, according to Mackey, Bultmann expressly holds, in a warning issued to Ernst Fuchs, that "'the kerygma does not permit any inquiry into the personal faith of the preacher' (that is, Jesus)" (164). Precisely because the faith demanded by the Christian kerygma is not the faith of Jesus in the coming reign of God but faith in Jesus himself as God's decisive act of salvation, we shall never understand, and we certainly can never justify, the kerygma's demand by historical inquiry into Jesus' own personal faith.

To this contention of Bultmann's, however, Mackey makes a twofold reply. In the first place, "if we range outside the context in which the word 'faith' itself is specifically used, to others which use an equivalent phrase, we shall see that the New Testament writers frequently and insistently present Jesus as a man of faith, and we shall then have all the warrant we could expect for doing so ourselves" (166). In the second place, "the conception of the historical Jesus as himself a man of faith can help rather than hinder our understanding of the conviction, expressed in the myth of Jesus, that in him we do indeed encounter the one true God . . . " (165). In fact, there is one reason that makes it more than plausible to look to Jesus' own personal faith both to explain and to justify the faith expressed in the myth about him. "This kind of faith, it seems, can only spread by contagion. Only carriers can truly give it to others" (169; cf. 196). In the end, Mackey argues, we can be brought to that experience of all life and existence as grace which is Christian faith only through the grace of another human person through whom we find ourselves forgiven, accepted, and served and in this way enabled and inspired to forgive, accept, and serve others. "And there is really no possibility of dissimulation here." For "power-seeking in service, like condescension in giving, or cowardly envy in forgiving, is too easily perceptible, if sometimes, unfortunately perceived too late, and no good comes of it, no sense of life and existence as grace, no faith or love, no hope" (170). Consequently, if we have in fact come to Christian faith, and if it really is to Jesus, finally, that we somehow owe our having done so, we must conclude to his own personal faith as its only sufficient ground. "So Jesus cherished all life and existence, and especially other people, as God's precious gift, and so, without ulterior motive, he accepted all and served their needs, and so enabled and inspired them to discover the treasure hidden in their lives. . . . The only alternative here is to see the human personality of Jesus as a purely passive mask for the dramatic speeches of divinity. And that neither the scriptures nor the great tradition allows us to do" (170–71).

There is no question that Mackey has Bultmann in mind, even if not exclusively, in what he thus characterizes as "the only alternative" to his position. In his view, faith either has its source and origin, under God, in the faith of the historical Jesus or else does not really arise out of history at all. Thus he speaks of Bultmann's thesis that "history and faith can find no common ground in research into the origins of Christianity" as "this new (and old) idea that faith, at least its source, is entirely above and beyond history, and that documents presenting faith are not therefore amenable to source-research of the normal rational kind" (44–45). In the same vein, he can ask a series of rhetorical questions about the origin of Christian faith and proclamation, only to observe, "Clearly Bultmann does not want such questions asked or answered" (255). But more even than this, Mackey claims that those who, like Bultmann, "force a dichotomy between faith and history are really the last of a long line of human beings who have given up on history" (256). Indeed, Bultmann's theory of the Christian faith devalues "the world of our historical experience" in the same way, even if not quite as much, as do "literal theories of special divine revelatory interventions, on the one hand, or absolute theories of fallen nature on the other" (256).

So far as Mackey is concerned, then, the issue between his position and Bultmann's is clear: either "our world and its history is itself the source of our faith in God" or else its source must be found in "some proclamation into the origin of which we may not even inquire" (256).

III

In turning now to criticism of Mackey's proposal, I wish to begin with his constructive position. Students of revisionary christology since Schleiermacher will readily agree, I believe, that the essentials of this position are hardly new.[4] And students of Bultmann's early work will be equally quick to recognize that it was an earlier version of the same position over against which he defined his own in his critical discussions with Wilhelm Herrmann and Emanuel Hirsch as well as Johannes Weiss.[5] Still, the very fact that Mackey develops his position explicitly as an alternative to Bultmann's makes clear that it is not simply the same as that of an earlier revisionary christology. Even if all the essentials of its claims are familiar enough, the arguments required to establish these claims today involve difficulties of their own, which are none the less serious for being in some respects new.

This is particularly true of the claim that the personal faith of Jesus himself is not outside the range of the historian. For all that Mackey says about the sources being adequate, indeed, providing "more than enough," to allow us to recover Jesus' faith, it is significant that he nowhere offers the least evidence or argument against one of the most secure conclusions of historical-critical study of these sources—namely, that even the earliest of them are all secondary and have the character of engaged witnesses of faith rather than disinterested historical reports. Of course, this is a literary conclusion about the character of the traditions redacted in the gospels, not a historical judgment about what can or cannot be known by controlled inferences from the traditions to the history lying behind them. But if it thus leaves room to use the sources for a historical inquiry into Jesus' faith, it also renders any such inquiry peculiarly problematic. Because all the sources are at best secondary and are witness and not reportage, any inference from them about Jesus himself can be controlled, if at all, only by yet another inference of exactly the same kind.

This can also be put by saying that one can never make any operational distinction between Jesus as he really was and Jesus as he is represented in the earliest of these sources. Because the only evidence one has for the first is strictly identical with whatever evidence one has for the second, any distinction one may make between them must either remain merely theoretical or else beg the question. But if this means, in general, that one can never talk historically about what Jesus said and did as distinct from what he was heard to have said and

[4] See S. Faut, *Die Christologie seit Schleiermacher. Ihre Geschichte und ihre Begründung* (Tübingen: Mohr-Siebeck, 1907).

[5] *Glauben und Verstehen I* (Tübingen: Mohr-Siebeck, 1933) 85–113, 245–67. Cf. also Hans Grass, "Die Christologie der neueren Systematischen Theologie. 19. Jahrhundert und Gegenwart," in idem and Werner Georg Kümmel, eds., *Jesus Christus. Das Christusverständnis im Wandel der Zeiten* (Marburg: Elwert, 1963) 109–21; and idem, *Christliche Glaubenslehre* (2 vols.; Stuttgart: Kohlhammer, 1973) I. 93–99.

seen to have done by those whose witness to him provides our only sources, it just as surely means that one can never talk historically about Jesus' own personal faith as distinct from such faith as he may have been understood to have had by these same earliest witnesses. To be sure, one might conceivably try to infer Jesus' faith indirectly from material authentically reporting his words and deeds. But not only would one then still be faced with the problem of distinguishing Jesus' own words and deeds from the sayings and actions attributed to him in the earliest witness, but one would confront the further difficulty of backing up the warrants required to license one's inference sufficiently to make them acceptable historical warrants.

Just how serious this difficulty is, is clear from the warrant Mackey invokes in asserting that there is really no possibility of dissembling faith. Not only does he quite fail to provide any evidence or argument for this assertion, but it is incredible on its face if one keeps in mind that what is meant by "faith" here is not particular words or deeds or even some more fundamental trait of observable behavior, but, rather, the utterly personal act of accepting one's own existence and all existence as grace. Clearly, any such act can be experienced by another even in principle only through its putative expressions, and of these one must always be able to say what Paul says of even the most radical expressions of love: even "if I give away all I have, and if I deliver my body to be burned," the possibility remains that I "have not love" (1 Cor 13:3). In short, there is really a possibility of dissimulation here, and Mackey's warrant is so far from being an acceptable license for historical inferences as to give every appearance of special pleading. But this means that, for all he shows to the contrary, the faith of Jesus *is* outside the historian's range and, since this is true in principle as well as in fact, no christology that supposedly gives expression to this faith as its historical source, his own included, can even possibly be explained or justified.

The same conclusion about the character of our sources as well as of the New Testament writings generally suffices to undermine the argument for another of Mackey's claims—to the effect, namely, that the New Testament writers provide all the warrant we could expect for presenting Jesus as himself a man of faith. Mackey actually offers two arguments for this claim. In addition to the argument mentioned above, that there are contexts in the New Testament such as the Epistle to the Hebrews where Jesus is implicitly presented as believing in God by describing him in equivalent terms as hearing and obeying God's word or will, he also seeks to show that in a passage like Gal 2:16 the original Greek usually translated so as to refer to the faith of which Jesus is the object could be read as easily and even more literally as referring to the personal faith of Jesus himself (163). The difficulty with both of these arguments, however, is that they ignore the conclusion overwhelmingly confirmed by historical-critical study that all the New Testament writings are, first and last, documents of faith and witness. Thus even if Mackey were to succeed in showing that their authors present Jesus, as he claims, "frequently and insistently" as a man of faith, the question would remain whether this in any way warranted his own talk of Jesus' faith as the one historical source of Christian faith and witness. It is one thing to bear witness to Jesus as the Christ because one experiences him to be a man of faith; it is another and very different thing to bear witness to Jesus as a man of faith because one believes him to be the Christ.

This difference becomes all the more significant if one takes seriously the rule already laid down that the personal faith of one human being can never be experienced by another except through its putative expressions from which it can never be certainly inferred. Assuming that the earliest witnesses' experience of Jesus could not have been an exception to this rule, one can only conclude that anything they may have said or implied about Jesus' faith had a very different import from that which Mackey's arguments presume it to have had. Far from justifying their christological assertion by appealing to its historical source, their talk about Jesus' faith could only have been one among a number of other ways of formulating this very assertion. And this conclusion becomes irresistible when one considers the obviously idealized way in which the New Testament writings actually speak of Jesus' faithfulness to his vocation and submission to God's will (Matt 4:1–11 par.; Mark 14:32–42), his godly fear and obedience (Heb 5:7–10), his exemplary endurance of suffering (1 Pet 2:21–25), or his sinlessness (Heb 4:15; 7:26–28). All such talk undoubtedly has the literary character of legend, being in every way comparable with the accounts of Jesus' miraculous conception and birth or of his equally miraculous appearances after death. But insofar as it itself is thus christology rather than an attempted historical justification thereof, it provides no warrant whatever for Mackey's attempt to justify christology historically by presenting Jesus as himself a person of faith.

This brings us to the other claim that Mackey makes in replying to Bultmann's contention that we can never understand, much less justify, the demand of the Christian kerygma by inquiring historically into Jesus' own personal faith. On the contrary, Mackey claims, the conception of Jesus as himself a person of faith can help rather than hinder our understanding of the belief expressed in the myth of Jesus that in him we meet the one, true God. Here again the difficulties involved in trying to establish Mackey's claim are serious.

Consider, first of all, his use of the old premise that Christian faith, or—since they are really one and the same—the distinctive faith of Jesus, can only be conveyed by contagion, in that one must catch it from a carrier who already has it. Obviously, if this premise were true without exception, one could establish the fact of Jesus' faith only by immediately raising the question about the carrier from which it, in turn, had to have been caught. But, then, if one were to allow this question by allowing that such a carrier could indeed be identified, Jesus would be relativized to simply one more in the intervening chain of carriers, and one would have to withdraw any claim that his faith is the unique source of the faith that others have caught from him. If, on the other hand, one were to try to uphold the claim for the uniqueness of Jesus' faith, one would have to disallow the question about its own source, thereby implying the falsity of the premise save insofar as it admitted of at least one notable exception. But if it were to admit of this one exception, it could presumably admit of any number of others, in which event Jesus' faith would not be the unique source of faith after all.

There is little question that Mackey's argument avoids the first horn of this dilemma. He at no point allows the question about the carrier of faith by whom Jesus himself was infected, and he clearly intends Jesus to be an exception to his premise, although, admittedly, he does not so formulate it as to allow for this exception. Thus, in arguing that "we can only sense ourselves and our world valued and cherished by God when we feel ourselves valued and cherished by others," he expressly distinguishes Jesus from "the rest of us" by insisting that "it is very likely that his power to value [others] went far beyond anyone's ability to value him" (170). Elsewhere this still qualified claim for Jesus' exceptional status gives way to such unqualified claims as that he "fully realized and actualized" the possibility of faith and that "he was no sinner" (238, 243; cf. 232). But it is just such unqualified claims, which, incidentally, no quest of the historical Jesus could ever verify, that reveal the difficulty of Mackey's argument; for if they enable him to avoid the second horn of the dilemma as well, by defeating the presumption that there could be any number of exceptions to the premise besides Jesus, they themselves are groundless claims for all that he says to support them. This is so, at any rate, unless one allows that they are perhaps tacitly supported by the very mythical belief that the conception of Jesus as himself a person of faith is supposed to help us understand.

It is evident that this conception can be of no help whatever in understanding that belief unless it is the conception of Jesus' faith as a unique personal faith. But, as I have shown, one cannot derive such a conception either from a quest of the historical Jesus or from the kind of talk about Jesus' faith that may be found in the New Testament. If, on the contrary, any claims for the uniqueness of Jesus' faith are simply one way, more or less adequate, of formulating the belief that he is the Christ, the difficulty of Mackey's argument is serious, indeed. Far from helping our understanding of the belief expressed in the myth of Jesus, the conception of Jesus as a man of faith must itself be helped by this very belief before it can be even so much as relevant to such understanding.

If this conception does not help our understanding, however, what about the other part of Mackey's claim that it does not hinder our understanding? To make good on this part of his claim he would have to show, as distinct from merely assuming, that being the unique man of faith that he takes Jesus to have been is the sufficient condition for truthfully asserting the belief about Jesus expressed in the myth. He would have to show this, I say, because, if this were not the case, if the belief about Jesus were grounded in anything other or more than his unique personal faith, to appeal, as Mackey does, simply to the conception of Jesus as having such faith in order to understand the belief would indeed hinder our understanding of it—namely, by confusing at best a partial explanation or justification with a complete one. As it happens, however, Mackey does not even begin to show that this most fundamental assumption of his position is well-founded. The sufficient proof of this is that he nowhere considers, much less succeeds in meeting, the objections that have long been urged against the same assumption when it has been made by others proposing an essentially similar position. Thus not only does he ignore Bultmann's repeated arguments against this assumption, but he does not even take account of the parallel arguments more recently advanced by at least one English-speaking theologian with whose work he otherwise seems to be familiar.[6]

According to these counterarguments, however, not even a Jesus whose faith was as unique as Mackey takes it to have been would be sufficient to explain or justify the belief expressed in the myth about him. At most, such a Jesus would be merely one more human being

[6] See J. Hick's two essays, "The Christology of D. M. Baillie," *SJTh* 11 (1958) 1–12; and "Christology at the Crossroads," in F. Healy, ed., *Prospect for Theology: Essays in Honour of H. H. Farmer* (London, 1966) 137–66, 233–34.

among others, on the same level as ourselves, even if first and foremost among us, whereas the whole point of the myth is that Jesus is infinitely more than a mere man, on the same level as God, even if also distinct from God as the one through whom God is decisively encountered. If this is undoubtedly the point of what Mackey calls "the full-grown myth" of Jesus' deity as formulated at Nicaea, it is not any less the point even of the original myth of Jesus' resurrection and the titles attributed to him in the earliest witness. For while this earliest form of the myth was indeed cast in terms drawn from Jewish religious tradition, and thus represented Jesus as in every way human, in no way divine, its point nonetheless was to place him on *God's* side of the relation between God and human beings generally, not on the side of human beings who more or less fully believe in God. As he whom God has made Messiah by raising him from the dead, Jesus is not merely a believer in God, not even the "original and originative" believer, but is rather the one through whom God has spoken and acted in a final decisive way to re-present the possibility of faith to all who would believe.

If such counterarguments are sound, however, and this really is the point of the myth of Jesus, this last difficulty of Mackey's argument is certainly not the least. By failing to show that the unique faith of the historical Jesus is the sufficient condition of making this essential point, he is open to the decisive objection of proposing a christology that at best makes another and very different point, and hence hinders rather than helps our understanding of what any christology is all about.

IV

But if Mackey's position is clearly untenable, is the only alternative the position he criticizes as Bultmann's? Must we locate the source of our faith in God, not in the Jesus of history, but in some proclamation into whose origin we may not even inquire? No, this is not our only alternative, because, as I now propose to show, Bultmann's real position is sufficiently different from the one Mackey attributes to him to be a third distinct possibility.

Two points may be made immediately about Mackey's criticisms. In the first place, to suggest as he does that Bultmann forbids inquiry into the origin of the Christian proclamation or regards documents of faith as not amenable to normal, rational source-research is not to describe Bultmann's position but to caricature it. Bultmann not only nowhere tries to keep questions about the origin of faith and proclamation from being asked or answered, but again and again asks and answers them himself—as he does, for instance, even in his criticism of the new questers, when he argues for a strict historical continuity between Jesus' own proclamation and the early church's message about Christ.[7] Likewise, one of the most characteristic themes of his theology is the "paradox" or "scandal" of the eschatological event, which lies precisely in the fact that the very phenomena that Christian faith proclaims as eschatological—Jesus himself, the apostles who proclaim him, and the church constituted by their proclamation—are all genuinely historical phenomena that are subject to "historical, sociological, and psychological examination" exactly like any other.[8] But if this means that Bultmann in no way exempts documents of faith from the same source-research that applies to all historical documents, it also means that he is unequivocal about the genuinely historical source of our faith insofar as it derives from the apostolic proclamation of the church. Therefore, Mackey is misleading, in the second place, when he represents Bultmann as forcing a dichotomy between faith and history and thus devaluing the world of our historical experience. Even if Bultmann were to maintain as simply as Mackey claims he does that the source of Christian faith is the kerygma, his unambiguous assertion of the historicity of the kerygma itself, both as the church's present proclamation and as the normative proclamation of the apostles, would falsify Mackey's claim that he asserts the essential independence of Christian faith and history.

The truth, however, is that Bultmann does not maintain in any such simple or unqualified way that the kerygma is the source of Christian faith. As a matter of fact, in his view, in contrast to the one for which Mackey criticizes him, any such tenet is evidently subject to two important qualifications.

The first of these becomes apparent in a highly instructive discussion of how the meaning of the cross as the salvation-event comes to be understood. If Mackey's criticism were to the point, one would naturally expect Bultmann simply to deny that there was ever any need to understand the historical Jesus in order to understand the significance of his cross. In fact, however, he precludes any such simple denial by explicitly distinguishing between our own situation today and that of

[7] *Das Verhältnis der urchristlichen Christusbotschaft zum historischen Jesus* (Heidelberg: Winter, 1960) 11–12, 15–16.

[8] "Neues Testament und Mythologie. Das Problem der Entmythologisierung der neutestamentlichen Verkündigung," in Hans-Werner Bartsch, ed., *Kerygma und Mythos* I (Hamburg: Evangelischer Verlag, 1951) 48.

the first proclaimers. If there is indeed no need for us to first understand the historical Jesus in order to understand the meaning of the cross, this is because we are already confronted with the Christian kerygma in which its meaning is explicitly proclaimed. It was otherwise, however, with those first proclaimers to whom we ultimately owe this very kerygma, since their only recourse was the historical Jesus. "They experienced the cross of the one with whom they had been bound in the living present. Out of this personal bond, in which the cross was an event in their own life, it became a question for them and disclosed to them its meaning."[9]

Interestingly enough, Bultmann refers here explicitly to "the historical Jesus" (den historischen Jesus), even if in other, closely parallel passages he expresses himself more adequately—for instance, by speaking simply of "facts of the past" that become "historical phenomena" (geschichtlichen Phänomenen) only by acquiring a meaning for a subject who exists in history and participates in it and, therefore, is "bound up with them in historical life."[10] Either way, however, his point is clear: it was through the first proclaimers' own immediate experience of the Jesus of history as a "fact of the past" that his cross first came to be understood as having decisive significance. And this interpretation is fully confirmed by what Bultmann says elsewhere on the same point:

> The decision to accept Jesus' having been sent that his 'disciples' had once made by 'following' him had to be made anew and radically in consequence of his crucifixion. The cross, so to say, raised once again the question of decision; for as little as it could call in question the what of his proclamation, so much it could and did make questionable the that of his proclamation—his legitimation, the claim that he was God's messenger bringing the final decisive word. The church had to overcome the scandal of the cross and did so with the faith of Easter.[11]

Of course, this first qualification that Bultmann makes of any claim that faith has its source simply in the kerygma is, in a way, self-evident. After all, the kerygma is a historical emergent whose source could only be found beyond itself in the immediate experience and faith of those to whom we owe it. But if Bultmann leaves no doubt that the experience and faith that are thematized in the kerygma are

[9] "Neues Testament und Mythologie," 43–44.

[10] *Glauben und Verstehen II* (Tübingen: Mohr-Siebeck, 1952) 229.

[11] *Theologie des Neuen Testaments* (Tübingen: Mohr-Siebeck, 1958) 47.

those of Good Friday and Easter, he is equally clear that neither the question of decision raised by the cross nor the answer given to this question by faith in the resurrection was completely new and unprecedented. In fact, he explicitly affirms in the passage just quoted that the cross raised "*once again*" the same question of decision that had already been raised by Jesus' proclamation and that the decision that had to be made anew and radically in consequence of his crucifixion was the same decision that the disciples had already made "*once*" by following him during his lifetime. In other words, in Bultmann's view, not only did the disciples' experience of the cross depend upon their prior experience of Jesus' life to disclose its meaning, but even the faith to which they came at Easter but renewed and radicalized the faith to which they had already come in accepting Jesus as sent by God.

It is only natural, then, that Bultmann's many discussions of the origin of christology typically point, first of all, not to the disciples' experience of Jesus' death and resurrection, but to their prior experience of his proclamation. More exactly, it is their experience of the *that* of Jesus' proclamation that Bultmann represents as christologically decisive. Thus, according to one typical account, Jesus appeared as a prophet and teacher proclaiming the imminent coming of God's reign and the radical demand of God's will. Although he presented no teaching about his own person, his summons to decision for or against his proclamation as God's own word in the last hour definitely implied a christology. This christology became explicit in the early community to the extent that it confessed that God had made Jesus Messiah and that as such he would soon come. Bultmann observes:

> This shows that the community understood Jesus' word—and this means not its timeless content of ideas, but his having spoken it and their having been addressed by it—as the decisive act of God. But this is also to say that their transmission of Jesus' proclamation could not consist in a simple reproduction of his ideas. Instead, the proclaimer had to become the one proclaimed. Precisely the *that* of his proclamation is decisive.[12]

Elsewhere Bultmann offers much the same account, only to formulate his distinction between the that and the what of Jesus' proclamation by also distinguishing between Jesus' "person" and his "personality." He argues:

[12] *Glauben und Verstehen I*, 204–5.

> Whether Jesus knew himself to be the Messiah or not is indifferent. It would only mean that he became conscious of the decisive character of his work in terms of a contemporary Jewish idea. But, of course, his summons to decision implies a christology, although neither as metaphysical speculation about a heavenly being nor as a character sketch of his personality as having a messianic consciousness. Rather, it is a christology that is proclamation or personal address. Therefore, if the early community designates Jesus as the Messiah, it expresses in its way that it has understood him. . . . The proclaimer had to become the one proclaimed because the decisive thing about his proclamation is its that, not his personality, but his person, its being here and now, its event, its commission, its personal address. In designating him the Messiah, the early community understands him as the decisive event, as the act of God, that inaugurates the new world.[13]

The significance of this passage, I submit, is to make clear that and why any distinction Bultmann makes between the Christian kerygma and the historical Jesus has nothing like the axiomatic status in his position that Mackey represents it as having. No doubt when Bultmann refers to our situation today, he uses this distinction to argue that our faith does indeed arise in response to the kerygma rather than the historical Jesus. But when he discusses the origin of christology in the experience of the first proclaimers, this distinction proves to be derived—namely, from the original distinction that he formulates either by distinguishing between the that and the what of Jesus' proclamation or by distinguishing between Jesus' person and his personality. Certainly, so far as these first Christians were concerned, the source of Christian faith was no more the kerygma than it was the historical Jesus, in the sense of the personality of Jesus endowed with messianic consciousness, the what of whose proclamation was nothing other than radicalized Jewish prophetism. Rather, the source of the Christian faith in which the kerygma had its origin was the person of Jesus, the that of whose proclamation was already understood by those who followed him to be the decisive act of God. Thus Bultmann can say that "the real content of the Easter faith that God has made the prophet and teacher of Jesus of Nazareth the Messiah" is "that Jesus' having come was itself the decisive event through which God has

[13] *Glauben und Verstehen I*, 265–66.

summoned his congregation, that this event itself was already eschatological occurrence."[14]

But even if Bultmann thus holds that the faith of the first proclaimers had its source in their immediate experience of the person of Jesus, has it not already become clear that he gives a very different account of the source of our faith today? Is not Mackey justified in his criticism at least to the extent that, so far as we are concerned, Bultmann allows the kerygma alone to be the source of our faith?

I should not wish to deny that there is a certain amount of evidence to which one could appeal in support of Mackey's criticism. As I have indicated, Bultmann distinguishes our situation today from that of the first proclaimers insofar as our faith arises in response to the kerygma rather than the historical Jesus. Moreover, there are even passages in which he expressly affirms that Jesus Christ can be encountered only in the kerygma and nowhere else. But whatever one is to finally make of this affirmation, one can hardly expect to understand it correctly except by interpreting these passages in the light of other things that Bultmann expressly says—in which case one will have to take account of his consistent teaching that even for us today there can be an existentialist interpretation of, and hence an existential encounter with, Jesus' own proclamation and that this proclamation at least implied Jesus' claim to be Christ. More important, however, is the fact that Bultmann's own understanding of the kerygma in no way allows it to be taken simply in itself independently of the Jesus to whom it bears witness. On the contrary, it remains entirely dependent for its authority on Jesus himself, and as the proclamation of his decisive significance for human existence the experience it mediates is an experience precisely of him. Consequently, when Bultmann takes the position that it is the kerygma rather than the historical Jesus that is the norm of christology, he is not denying but affirming that the primal source of Christian faith even for us today is Jesus himself.

This becomes clear from his repeated statements that it is precisely Jesus as a genuinely historical event by which the present proclamation of the kerygma is authorized or legitimated. Significantly, Mackey not only completely ignores such statements but, by focusing on another statement of Bultmann's in isolation from them, gives his readers to understand that Bultmann simply contrasts legitimating with faith, "so that one rules out the other . . ." (304, n. 19).

[14] *Theologie des Neuen Testaments*, 45. Cf. also *Jesus* (Berlin: Deutsche Bibliothek, 1926) 197–98, where Bultmann argues that the earliest community confessed Jesus to be the Messiah "on the authority of his words."

Bultmann does indeed contrast legitimating and faith as mutually exclusive in the sense that the kerygma's existential assertion that Jesus is the Christ logically could not be legitimated by any empirical assertion about the historical Jesus. But to rule out legitimating the kerygma in this sense is not to rule out legitimating it altogether, and there is another sense in which Bultmann repeatedly states that the kerygma can and must be legitimated.

Thus, in arguing at one point that New Testament theology performs a necessary theological task, he reasons as follows: "Since the kerygma of today acquires its legitimation from the Christ-event of the past, present preaching and systematic theology with it have need of a critical control that secures its identity with the apostolic preaching—namely, New Testament theology."[15] If this statement confirms how seriously Mackey misunderstands Bultmann in criticizing him for making faith completely independent of historical inquiry, it also makes clear how different Bultmann's theological norm is from Mackey's. What must be secured if present preaching is to be legitimate, he holds, is its identity with "the apostolic preaching," not its identity with the preaching or faith of the historical Jesus. But it is no less clear from this statement that even the apostolic preaching is the *primary norm* of the kerygma of today, not the *primal source* from which it acquires its legitimation insofar as it is identical in substance with the apostolic preaching. The only primal source of its legitimation, Bultmann affirms, is "the Christ-event of the past," by which all preaching, including the uniquely normative preaching of the apostles, is authorized or legitimated.

But, clearly, what Bultmann here refers to as "the Christ-event of the past" is one and the same with what he speaks of elsewhere as "the that of Jesus' proclamation," or "Jesus' person, its being here and now, its event, its commission, its personal address." Thus, in interpreting Johannine theology, he can say that Jesus is there represented as himself the word of Christian proclamation because "this word in which judgment and forgiveness, death and life, become event is established, authorized, and legitimated by the event Jesus."[16] And he interprets Paul's teaching that the new age becomes a reality in the kerygma and in the faith that works by love as affirming that this all happens precisely "*through the historical Jesus* (den geschichtlichen Jesus). But not through the 'personality,' whether understood as a character or as a

[15] "Theologie als Wissenschaft," in *Protokoll der Tagung "Alter Marburger" 2.-5. Januar 1979 in Hofgeismar* (Berlin, 1979) 17–18.

[16] *Glauben und Verstehen I*, 292.

'figure' embodying certain ideas, so that the new age would be a new epoch in the history of culture. Christ is accessible only through the kerygma, and the new age is to be seen only in faith." Even so, Bultmann insists, when Paul speaks of the obedience and love of Christ, referring thereby to the pre-existent one rather than to any attributes of the historical Jesus (des historischen Jesus), he intends nothing other than the service performed for us by "Jesus, the historical person" (Jesus, die geschichtliche Person). For "'the obedience' of Christ is the fact of his historical person in its service to us, and his 'love' is God's saving act in him. . . ."[17]

Rightly understood, the present proclamation of the kerygma is not some other source of faith to be taken in itself independently of the Jesus of history, but, rather, the very means by which he himself can be experienced here and now as faith's only primal source. Accordingly, Bultmann can say that the word of God is "not the mysterious saying of some oracle but sober proclamation of the person and destiny of Jesus of Nazareth in their significance as history of salvation."[18] Earlier in the same context he explains more fully what he means by this by speaking of "genuine historical understanding" (echt geschichtliches Verständnis) of Jesus' crucifixion. "It is precisely not to mythological but to historical (geschichtlichem) understanding that the historical (historische) event discloses itself as the salvation-event, insofar as genuine historical understanding understands a historical event in its significance. At bottom, mythological talk seeks to do nothing other than to express the significance of the historical event. In the significance that belongs to it, the historical (historische) event of the cross has created a new historical (geschichtliche) situation; the proclamation of the cross as the salvation-event asks the hearer whether he is willing to appropriate this meaning, whether he is willing to be crucified with Christ."[19] In other words, the present proclamation originates in the kind of immediate experience of Jesus that Bultmann calls "genuine historical understanding" of his significance; and in proclaiming him to be the salvation-event, it seeks to do nothing other than to express this very significance, thereby mediating to the hearer the same kind of experience of Jesus himself. With good reason, then, Bultmann can accept the statement often made as a criticism of his view that it is in the kerygma that Jesus is risen. For, rightly understood, this statement does indeed presuppose that the

[17] *Glauben und Verstehen I*, 212–13.
[18] "Neues Testament und Mythologie," 48.
[19] "Neues Testament und Mythologie," 43.

kerygma itself is eschatological occurrence, but what it affirms is "that Jesus is really present in the kerygma, that it is *his* word that encounters the hearer in the kerygma."[20]

The evidence is thus doubly clear that Bultmann's theology is anything but the kind of "kerygma-theology" that Mackey, like so many others, attributes to him. Not only does he clearly point to the apostles' immediate experience of Jesus' person as the primal source of their original and originating faith and preaching, but he is also clear in insisting that even our own faith today, in response to the proclamation normed by their preaching, has its only primal source in the same kind of experience of Jesus himself. Of course, our experience of Jesus, being mediated by theirs, can only be a mediate, not an immediate, experience, for exactly the same reasons that would apply to our experience of any other fact of the past that we could not possibly experience except through the experience of others. But provided that the proclamation to which we respond is indeed normed by the apostles' preaching, which itself arises out of their immediate experience of Jesus' person, the primal source of our experience no less than of theirs is not the kerygma but precisely and only the Jesus of history.

To recognize this, however, is to understand why the real issue between a position like Mackey's and Bultmann's very different position is not at all as Mackey represents it. It is not at all the issue of *whether* the Jesus of history is the source of our faith in God; it is entirely the issue of *what* Jesus of history is rightly said to be the source of our faith. Is it, as Mackey contends, the Jesus of history whom we first come to know only more or less probably by historical inquiry back behind the preaching of the apostles as well as of all other Christians who follow after them? Or is it, rather, as Bultmann holds, the Jesus of history whom we already know most certainly through the same apostolic preaching as well as all later Christian preaching insofar as it is normed by that of the apostles? Either way, we clearly have to do with the Jesus of history, even if in the one way exactly as in the other our experience of him today is and must be a mediated experience. Nevertheless, there remains the issue—and it is a rock-bottom, fundamental issue—between a position like Mackey's, for which the apostolic preaching that mediates our experience is forced to function as the primary source from which the Jesus of history must still be reconstructed, and a position such as Bultmann's for which this same earliest preaching is allowed to function as the primary norm through which the Jesus of history is even now to be

[20] *Das Verhältnis der urchristlichen Christusbotschaft zum historischen Jesus*, 27.

encountered. In the one case, we have to do with the Jesus of history in his being in himself then and there in the past, while in the other case we have to do with the Jesus of history in his meaning for us here and now in the present.

Of course, to show, as I have tried to do, that this is the real issue that Bultmann poses for most other proposals in revisionary christology, both earlier and more recent, is not to answer the question of whether his way of resolving this issue really leads to the future. Perhaps when it is freed from misunderstandings and seen for what it is, it will prove to be as untenable a position as Mackey's, or, at any rate, less adequate than some other alternative that is open to us. But if Mackey's criticisms are at all representative—and if they fail in being so, surely it is only in being more rather than less understanding of Bultmann's intentions than most others—the grave weakness of the larger discussion of Bultmann's position up to now is that this further question of its adequacy has hardly been fairly raised, much less finally answered.

No one who knew Rudolf Bultmann could doubt that he was serenely confident about the future of his contribution, believing as he did with Paul that we cannot do anything against the truth but only for it.[21] But in fairness both to him and to the future of revisionary christology, those of us who now bear responsibility for this future simply must reconsider the question of their relationship. Certainly, he would have asked for nothing more; and anyone who owes him as much as I do can settle for nothing less.

[21] "Ist Jesus auferstanden wie Goethe?" *Der Spiegel*, 25 July 1966, 42.

Helmut Koester

Early Christianity from the Perspective of the History of Religions: Rudolf Bultmann's Contribution

I

Few would doubt that Rudolf Bultmann's most lasting accomplishment is his *Theology of the New Testament.* It will remain as our century's most perceptive and enlightening theological interpretation of Christianity's basic document. However, what guided Bultmann on his path to the completion of this work was, in my opinion, the study during several decades that was devoted to the investigation of the religious environment of the New Testament in the tradition of the history-of-religions school. It appears to me that much of this scholarly work of Rudolf Bultmann either has simply been taken for granted or was not even mentioned in the process of the ongoing debate about the theological significance of his contribution.

Let me begin to illustrate this with a few reminiscences about my experience as a student of theology in the years immediately following World War II.

Even after several semesters in Rudolf Bultmann's lectures and seminars, if someone had asked me, "Who are the history-of-religions scholars at the university of Marburg?" I would not have named Bultmann. There were two students of Rudolf Otto on the faculty, both teaching systematic theology. And there was Friedrich Heiler, though he was then a member of the arts-and-sciences faculty (until 1948). But Bultmann?—No!

There are several reasons for this negative answer:

1. To judge from the lecture courses which Bultmann offered, there could be no doubt that he was a New Testament scholar and theologian. It was John's Gospel, Romans, 1 Corinthians, 2 Corinthians, New Testament Theology—and then the cycle of his courses began again with John's Gospel. They were exegetical and theological

lectures with minute exegetical detail which were difficult to understand without the Novum Testamentum Graece in front of each student in class. There were explanations of crucial terms with references to other biblical and to nonbiblical materials: Greek philosophy, Stoic moralists, Gnostic texts. And then came the great moments in class when the student's patience was rewarded with these crystal-clear summaries of the meaning of the text, its theological significance, and the consequences for the understanding of Christian faith and life. It was for this reason that hundreds of students came to Rudolf Bultmann's classes in these last years before his retirement, including large numbers from other faculties.

2. At that time Rudolf Bultmann was publishing *Theology of the New Testament.*[1] In the year of the appearance of the first fascicle of this work (1948), the volume of collected essays *Glauben und Verstehen*[2] also became available again in the bookstores.[3] There are no examples of Bultmann's history-of-religions works among the articles of this volume, nor in any of the subsequent volumes of *Glauben und Verstehen.*[4] Unfortunately, there is no preface to any of these volumes of collected essays. The author does not tell us why these particular essays were chosen rather than any of the more exegetical and historical articles of the earlier period of the author's scholarly endeavors. The dust jacket of volume 3 of *Glauben und Verstehen* says that these essays allow the reader to have a look "into the workshop of an important theological thinker," and the dust jacket of volume 4 reveals: "In all these contributions of Rudolf Bultmann the same theme is dealt with: what it means to live historically as a human being, i.e., to exist while one lives on the basis of decisions."

In this way Rudolf Bultmann was presented at that time—not as a history-of-religions scholar. The *Theologie des Neuen Testaments* and *Glauben und Verstehen* were the works which were available and these were the works which students read first of all at that time.

The impression that Rudolf Bultmann was primarily a theologian, albeit a biblical theologian, was further reinforced by the "Demythologizing Debate" which was occupying everyone in the late forties and

[1] *Theologie des Neuen Testaments* (Tübingen: Mohr-Siebeck, 1st fascicle 1948, 2d fascicle 1951, 3d fascicle 1953).

[2] First published: Tübingen: Mohr-Siebeck, 1933; later reprinted as *Glauben und Verstehen I.*

[3] During the first years after the war almost no previously published book was available in any of the bookstores.

[4] Vol. 2 was published in 1952, vol. 3 in 1960, and vol. 4 in 1965; all volumes are published in Tübingen by Mohr-Siebeck.

early fifties. Scholars from many theological disciplines became involved in this debate, even philosophers. But, aside from some discussion of Bultmann's use of the term "myth," perspectives of the history-of-religions school did not play any role in this debate. Even exegetical details were not discussed very much, although Bultmann's major exegetical works were soon reprinted, often with an *Ergänzungsheft*. But it took almost another twenty years before Bultmann's most important essays on Hellenistic history of religion were also reprinted in a volume of collected essays: *Exegetica*, edited by Erich Dinkler.[5]

II

It is interesting to note that many of Rudolf Bultmann's works became available in the English-speaking world in exactly the opposite sequence of their original publication. To be sure, an English translation of the small volume *Die Erforschung der synoptischen Evangelien* (1930) was published in English translation as early as 1934,[6] and the same year witnessed the English publication of Bultmann's *Jesus*.[7] But the real impact of Bultmann's work on the English-speaking world began in 1951 with the publication of the *Theology of the New Testament*.[8] In the year of the publication of volume 2 of the *Theology of the New Testament* the second volume of *Glauben und Verstehen* appeared as *Essays, Philosophical and Theological*.[9] Two years later Bultmann's Gifford Lectures were published in England under the title *History and Eschatology*[10] and in the United States under the title *The Presence of Eternity*.[11] In the following year the Shaffer Lectures *Jesus Christ and Mythology*, delivered in 1951 at Yale Divinity School, appeared in the United States.[12] It is not surprising that the collection of essays in

[5] Rudolf Bultmann, *Exegetica: Aufsätze zur Erforschung des Neuen Testaments*, ausgewählt, eingeleitet und herausgegeben von Erich Dinkler (Tübingen: Mohr-Siebeck, 1967).

[6] Rudolf Bultmann and Karl Kundsin, *Form Criticism: Two Essays on New Testament Research* (trans. Frederick C. Grant; Willett, Clark & Company, 1934; New York: Harper, 1962).

[7] *Jesus and the Word*, trans. Louise Pettibone Smith (New York: Scribners, 1934).

[8] Trans. Kendrick Grobel (New York: Scribners, vol. 1, 1951; vol. 2, 1955).

[9] Trans. James C. G. Greig (London: SCM, 1955).

[10] Edinburgh: University Press, 1957.

[11] New York: Harper, 1957; in this case, the German edition, *Geschichte und Eschatologie* (Tübingen: Mohr-Siebeck, 1958), was published a year after the English edition.

[12] New York: Scribners, 1958; the German edition *Jesus Christus und die Mythologie* was not published until 1964.

English translation which Schubert Ogden published in the year 1960 under the title *Existence and Faith*[13] had the explicit intention to introduce Bultmann as a theological thinker, not primarily as an exegete and historian of religion. This volume indeed includes two of the exegetical articles which have never been reprinted in the German volumes of *Glauben und Verstehen* ("Romans 7 and the Anthropology of Paul," and "Ignatius and Paul"), but the insightful introduction of the editor barely mentions Bultmann's significance as an interpreter of ancient texts. Schubert Ogden writes,[14]

> In Bultmann's case . . . what constitutes the inner integrity of all that he really intends to say is his affirmation of the "infinite qualitative difference" between time and eternity in its several negative and positive implications.

One would hardly suspect that these words characterize the leading New Testament scholar of our century.

The major exegetical works of Rudolf Bultmann, though written before the publication of his *Theologie des Neuen Testaments*, appeared in English translation only after the English translations of his theological and philosophical writings, namely, *The History of the Synoptic Tradition* in 1963,[15] and the *Commentary on the Gospel of John* in 1971.[16] However, the collected essays *Exegetica* which Erich Dinkler published in 1967 have not yet been translated into English. Yet, in particular the essays dealing with the background of the Gospel of John, originally published in 1923,[17] 1925,[18] and 1928–1930,[19] Bultmann's response to Ernst Percy[20] of 1940,[21] and his review of Karl Holl's

[13] New York: Meridian, 1960.

[14] In Rudolf Bultmann, *Existence and Faith*, 14.

[15] Trans. J. Marsh (Oxford: Blackwell).

[16] Philadelphia: Westminster.

[17] "Der religionsgeschichtliche Hintergrund des Prologs zum Johannes-Evangelium," in ΕΥΧΑΡΙΣΤΗΡΙΟΝ: *Hermann Gunkel zum 60. Geburtstag* (2 vols.; FRLANT 36; Göttingen: Vandenhoeck & Ruprecht, 1923) 2. 3–26 = *Exegetica*, 10–35.

[18] "Die Bedeutung der neuerschlossenen mandäischen und manichäischen Quellen für das Verständnis des Johannesevangeliums," *ZNW* 24 (1925) 100–146 = *Exegetica*, 55–104.

[19] "Untersuchungen zum Johannesevangelium," *ZNW* 27 (1928) 113–63; *ZNW* 29 (1930) 169–92 = *Exegetica*, 124–97.

[20] *Untersuchungen über den Ursprung der johanneischen Theologie: Zugleich ein Beitrag zur Frage nach der Entstehung des Gnostizismus* (Lund: Gleerupska, 1939).

[21] "Johanneische Schriften und Gnosis," *Orientalische Literaturzeitung* 43 (1940) 150–75 = *Exegetica*, 230–54. One essay that appeared much later, published after World War II but probably written earlier, should probably be added to the list of

Urchristentum und Religionsgeschichte,[22] are works that have become increasingly significant in the present situation of scholarship, especially in the United States with its large number of scholars who are involved in the publication, translation, and interpretation of the Gnostic documents of the Nag Hammadi Library, and where the instruction in the history, phenomenology, and sociology of religion has become such an important part of the curriculum of colleges, universities, and theological schools.

These essays and reviews, after rereading them now, more than half a century after their original publication, strike me as methodologically extremely significant and well worth a critical reconsideration. In this context, one should also reconsider the history-of-religions works which Rudolf Bultmann inspired among his doctoral students of those early years of his teaching career at Marburg, although I shall not deal with them in this essay.

III

In his autobiographical reflections, Rudolf Bultmann names as his most influential theological teachers the church historian Karl Müller in Tübingen, Hermann Gunkel and Adolf von Harnack in Berlin, and Adolf Jülicher, Johannes Weiss, and Wilhelm Herrmann in Marburg. It was Johannes Weiss who inspired Bultmann's dissertation *Der Stil der paulinischen Predigt und die kynisch-stoische Diatribe*.[23] By the time Bultmann had completed his dissertation, Johannes Weiss had left Marburg to occupy a chair in Heidelberg, and his successor Wilhelm Heitmüller accepted the dissertation in the year 1910.

Both Johannes Weiss and Wilhelm Heitmüller belonged to what had come to be called the *Religionsgeschichtliche Schule*; indeed, Johannes Weiss must be considered as one of its founders. It is doubtful, however, whether one should really use the term "school" in its technical sense. Rather, it was a new beginning in a circle of young students and scholars at the University of Göttingen in the last two decades of the 19th century, all students of Albrecht Ritschl, the most towering figure of liberal theology in the second half of the last century. In his work *Die christliche Lehre von der Rechtfertigung und*

---

these history-of-religions works of Rudolf Bultmann: "Zur Geschichte der Lichtsymbolik im Altertum," *Philologus* 97 (1948) 1–36 = *Exegetica*, 323–55.

[22] *ThR*, n.s. 4 (1932) 1–21; not included in *Exegetica*.

[23] FRLANT 13; Göttingen: Vandenhoeck & Ruprecht, 1910.

Versöhnung,[24] Ritschl had created the classical writing of German liberal theology with its central evolutionary concept that the kingdom of God, as it was proclaimed by Jesus, is the divine design that would find its fulfillment through the establishment of moral law among humankind. An impressive number of leading theologians of the following generation were deeply influenced by Ritschl (Adolf von Harnack, Wilhelm Herrmann, Emil Schürer, Martin Rade, and others).

But several members of this circle of younger scholars in Göttingen made discoveries, primarily through their work in biblical exegesis, which were to present a fundamental challenge to Albrecht Ritschl's understanding of the Bible in general, and in particular to his interpretation of Jesus' preaching of the kingdom of God. Later, these younger scholars became known as the *Religionsgeschichtliche Schule*: Hermann Gunkel (born 1862, in Göttingen until 1889), William Wrede (born 1859, in Göttingen until 1893), Wilhelm Bousset (born 1865, remained in Göttingen as *Privatdozent* until the time of World War I), Ernst Troeltsch (born 1865, in Göttingen until 1892), and Johannes Weiss (born 1863, in Göttingen until 1895). Johannes Weiss, who was Albrecht Ritschl's son-in-law, in his book *Die Predigt Jesu vom Reiche Gottes* (published 1892, three years after Ritschl's death), presented the most direct attack upon the biblical basis of the theology of his teacher and father-in-law: Jesus' preaching of the kingdom of God was eschatological; Jesus expected the kingdom as divine miracle of the future that had no relationship to the moral perfection of humankind.

What the "members" of the *Religionsgeschichtliche Schule* had discovered would change the direction of biblical studies fundamentally. Other scholars were soon drawn into the sphere of influence of the initial discovery: Ulrich von Wilamowitz-Moellendorff (he taught in Göttingen from 1882–97), Julius Wellhausen (came to Göttingen in 1892),[25] Rudolf Otto (came to Göttingen in 1897), and elsewhere Albrecht Dieterich (1866–1908), student of the classical philologian Hermann Usener (1834–1905)[26] in Bonn, forcefully promoted the history-of-religions investigation of Hellenistic materials.

It may be useful to summarize briefly the new insights of these scholars, in order to evaluate Rudolf Bultmann's work as a scholar of

[24] 13 vols., 1870–74.

[25] He had been in Göttingen as a student in 1862–65 and as a *Privatdozent* in 1870–72—well before the beginnings of the *Religionsgeschichtliche Schule*.

[26] Usener was one of the first scholars in Germany to offer lectures on *Allgemeine Religionsgeschichte*.

the history of religions. They can be briefly characterized as follows:

1) The concepts of the Bible are not moral and intellectual, but mythical and eschatological.
2) Religion, and especially early Christianity, is syncretistic in character.
3) Cult and liturgy are the center of the religious experience of people (not literature and theological concepts).
4) Folklore and oral traditions are the instruments of the transmission of religious knowledge.
5) The central religious experience is essentially irrational.
6) The quest for the understanding of "religion" must transcend the limitations of any specific religion or theology.

When Rudolf Bultmann was a student in the first decade of the 20th century, the new insights of the *Religionsgeschichtliche Schule* had already been widely publicized, but its founders were still occupying important teaching positions in several universities, and Bultmann had studied under more than one of these scholars. But he had also been exposed to the liberal theology of Ritschl's students and friends (Wilhelm Herrmann and Adolf von Harnack). When he was in Marburg as a *Privatdozent* until 1916,[27] he had established a close association with Ritschl's student Martin Rade, the editor of the leading journal of liberal theology, *Die Christliche Welt*, and he himself became a member of the group "Freunde der christlichen Welt." When he returned to teach in Marburg in 1921, after several years at the University of Breslau (where he was a colleague of Rudolf Otto) and a year at the University of Giessen as the successor of Wilhelm Bousset (1920–21), he followed his *Doktorvater* Wilhelm Heitmüller who had accepted a call to Bonn. In the following year, his teacher Wilhelm Herrmann died and Rudolf Otto became his successor as professor of systematic theology. Adolf Jülicher retired a year later (1923). But in the year 1922, Martin Heidegger had moved to Marburg, and it seems that the association between Bultmann and Heidegger was established very quickly. This is the time in which Bultmann began to write his most important essays on the history-of-religions background of the New Testament.

In the earlier period, the influence of the *Religionsgeschichtliche Schule* is mostly visible in the works devoted to the investigations of nonliterary patterns of communication and transmission. This is, of course,

[27] He had written his *Habilitationsschrift*, submitted in 1912, under the supervision of the liberal historical-critical New Testament scholar and church historian Adolf Jülicher on "Die Exegese des Theodor von Mopsuestia."

first evident in Bultmann's dissertation on the style of Pauline preaching and its relationship to the rhetorical style of the Cynic preacher.[28] But Bultmann's major work that fulfills this part of the program of the *Religionsgeschichtliche Schule* is his fundamental work on the form criticism of the Synoptic Gospels, *Die Geschichte der Synoptischen Tradition*.[29] This book was written during Bultmann's years in Breslau (1916–20) and is dedicated to Wilhelm Heitmüller.

Rudolf Bultmann was never actively involved in pursuing the more universalistic ambitions of the history-of-religions program, that is, searching for the underlying common denominator of all specific religions and theologies. Nor did he accept any definition of the religious experience as fundamentally irrational. Of course, he knew that there are irrational, ecstatic, and mystical religious phenomena; but he would never allow these to govern the definition of Christian faith. There are numerous reflections of Bultmann on this subject. A statement from his "Autobiographical Reflections" summarizes his position well:

> It seemed to me that in this new theological movement (dialectical theology) it was rightly recognized . . . that the Christian faith is not a phenomenon of the history of religion, that it does not rest on a "religious *a priori*" (Troeltsch), and that therefore theology does not have to look upon it as a phenomenon of religious or cultural history.[30]

It is clear that there could be no common ground with Bultmann's colleague Rudolf Otto who had come to Marburg as the successor of Wilhelm Herrmann shortly after Bultmann's move from Giessen to Marburg. In his "Autobiographical Reflections," Bultmann mentions the "oppositions" within the theological faculty at Marburg, "especially the tension between Rudolf Otto and myself, . . . (which) stirred even the students and led to lively discussions."[31]

But Bultmann was fascinated by the history-of-religions discovery of the predominance of myth and mythological language in the New Testament and of the syncretistic character of early Christianity. As he began to prepare his commentary on the Gospel of John, the relationship of the message of this Gospel to its syncretistic environment and,

[28] *Der Stil der paulinischen Predigt und die kynisch-stoische Diatribe*, see above, n. 23.

[29] FRLANT 29; Göttingen: Vandenhoeck & Ruprecht, 1921; 2d ed., 1931; further eds. followed in 1957, 1958, and 1962; for the English translation, see above, n. 15.

[30] *Existence and Faith*, 288.

[31] Ibid., 286.

more specifically, to Gnostic mythology became the agenda for a series of publications in which Bultmann most clearly demonstrates that he was a student of the *Religionsgeschichtliche Schule.* This period of Bultmann's work also generated a renewed interest in the study of the religious environment of early Christianity among his students. Several dissertations written at Marburg during these years deal with this question, particularly with Gnosticism: Heinrich Schlier, *Religionsgeschichtliche Untersuchungen zu den Ignatiusbriefen,*[32] Ernst Käsemann, *Leib und Leib Christi,*[33] Günther Bornkamm, *Mythos und Legende in den apokryphen Thomasakten,*[34] and finally Hans Jonas, *Gnosis und spätantiker Geist.*[35]

In the first of these essays on the history-of-religions background of the Johannine Prologue,[36] the text of John 1 sets the stage for the inquiry. The problem is defined on the basis of peculiar features of this text, as compared to other texts from the early Christian period. In the case of the Fourth Gospel, of course, comparison with the Synoptic Gospels often serves the purpose of recognizing Johannine peculiarities more clearly. In this respect, Bultmann differs from Richard Reitzenstein who begins, in his *Hellenistic Mystery Religions,*[37] with the statement of a general assessment of the topic. Bultmann is, therefore, much more closely allied to Eduard Norden whose works[38] formulate the topic and problematic of the investigation on the basis of a particular text, namely Acts 17 and Virgil's *Fourth Eclogue,* respectively. It is only consistent with this starting point that Bultmann's comparative material is the reconstruction of a text, originally "Gnostic" in his opinion, for which he can adduce numerous parallels, primarily from Jewish wisdom literature.

[32] BZNW 8; Giessen: Töpelmann, 1929; see also his *Habilitationsschrift, Christus und die Kirche im Epheserbrief* (BhTh 6; Tübingen: Mohr-Siebeck, 1930).

[33] BhTh; Tübingen: Mohr-Siebeck, 1933; see also idem, *Das wandernde Gottesvolk* (FRLANT 55; Göttingen: Vandenhoeck & Ruprecht, 1938; 2d ed. 1959).

[34] FRLANT 49; Göttingen: Vandenhoeck & Ruprecht, 1933.

[35] Vol. 1 (FRLANT 51; Göttingen: Vandenhoeck & Ruprecht, 1934); vol. 2 was set in type 1934–35, but published only twenty years later (FRLANT 63; Göttingen: Vandenhoeck & Ruprecht, 1954).

[36] *Exegetica,* 10–35; originally published in 1923.

[37] Pittsburgh Theological Monograph Series 15; Pittsburgh: Pickwick, 1978; English translation of *Die hellenistischen Mysterienreligionen nach ihren Grundgedanken und Wirkungen* (3d ed. of 1927; Darmstadt: Wissenschaftliche Buchgesellschaft, 1956).

[38] *Agnostos Theos: Untersuchungen zur Formengeschichte religiöser Rede* (1913; Darmstadt: Wissenschaftliche Buchgesellschaft, 1956); idem, *Die Geburt des Kindes: Geschichte einer religiösen Idee* (1930; Darmstadt: Wissenschaftliche Buchgesellschaft, 1958).

Bultmann's essay of 1925[39] on the relevance of the new Mandaean and Manichaean Texts for the interpretation of the Gospel of John is also primarily text oriented. It makes the "riddle of the Gospel of John" the primary topic of the investigation. Specific texts from the Gospel of John set the stage for the detailed comparison with equally specific parallels from Mandaean and other literatures. It is clear that Bultmann works primarily as an exegete. The result of his investigation is the call for the reconstruction of the source which the author of the Gospel of John must have used in the construction of his discourses. As is well known, Bultmann's interpretation of these parts of the Gospel of John in his later commentary[40] depends on the assumption that such a source existed, and Bultmann's student Heinz Becker has indeed produced a very interesting reconstruction of this hypothetical source.[41]

However, some problems begin to appear in this second essay, though I do not think that these problems must be seen primarily in the widely criticized hypothesis of this Johannine *Redenquelle.* On the contrary, new texts, such as the *Dialogue of the Savior* from the Nag Hammadi Library, may indeed lead us back to Bultmann's original assumption that the Johannine discourses and dialogues rested on some kind of written source (or sources). Moreover, this source was most probably a Gnostic document. The real problem with Bultmann's approach is, in my opinion, a different one.

Bultmann departs to a certain degree from a strictly textual approach. After briefly reporting the result of Richard Reitzenstein's reconstruction of the redeemer myth of the primordial Anthropos, Bultmann introduces his own investigation by saying, "I will now demonstrate that this myth lies at the base of the Gospel of John."[42] To what degree the investigation is now determined by the general construct of this redeemer myth, and to what degree it is actually informed by the exegetical investigation of these Mandaean and Manichaean texts is, therefore, not always clear. The dilemma is *not* that the source for the Johannine discourses is reconstructed from materials which have been composed several centuries later. Bultmann is, of course, quite aware of this, and he is capable of adducing impressive

[39] See above, n. 18.

[40] Rudolf Bultmann, *Das Evangelium des Johannes* (KEK; Göttingen: Vandenhoeck & Ruprecht, 1941); for the English translation see above, n. 16.

[41] *Die Reden des Johannesevangeliums und der Stil der gnostischen Offenbarungsrede* (FRLANT 68; Göttingen: Vandenhoeck & Ruprecht, 1956).

[42] *Exegetica*, 55.

evidence from earlier sources, such as the *Odes of Solomon*, in order to support credibly the existence of the hypothetical source at a much earlier date. But the leading principle of the textual reconstruction is a theoretical construct that can be seriously criticized.[43]

That Bultman uses this myth only as a general concept of the religious milieu at the time of early Christianity has some further consequences which become visible, if one considers the interpretation of the Gospel of John itself: the question of the *Sitz im Leben* is not posed in sufficient specificity. We do not learn much about the particular function and purpose of the hypothetical source in which this myth has found its expression. Rather, the interpretation of its meaning does not go beyond the reflections about the more general religious ideas which dominate this type of mythical thinking: the fate of the divine soul, the call from beyond, and the redemption and the return of the soul to its heavenly origin. Since Bultmann correctly recognizes that the author of the Fourth Gospel is critical of the mythical description of the soul's fate in this process of fall and redemption, the reinterpretation of this mythical material becomes so radically reduced to the "that" (*dass*) of the revelation. There is hardly any alternative as long as the function of this mythical Gnostic source is only understood in such general terms. But the quest for the *Sitz im Leben* must reconstruct not only the mythical-religious dimension of the Gnostic source, but also its political, social, and communal function. It is possible to be more specific: the source must have been the bearer of a Gnostic message which was very much alive in Palestinian and Syrian Judaism; and it was used by the author of the Fourth Gospel at a time when his own community was trying to answer the question of its place in Judaism (or Israel)—quite likely also a political problem. What role does the critical interpretation of a Gnostic-Jewish document play in that particular historical situation?

If the more recent efforts of the interpretation of the texts from Nag Hammadi simply lead us to the substitution of a better, while ostensibly older, Gnostic source, we shall have failed the test of this question. It is not enough to point to Jewish baptist sects in Syria and Palestine in general as the place of origin for this source. The interpretation of

[43] See, e.g., Carsten Colpe, *Die religionsgeschichtliche Schule: Darstellung und Kritik ihres Bildes vom gnostischen Erlösermythus* (FRLANT 78; Göttingen: Vandenhoeck & Ruprecht, 1961). Bultmann's essay of 1925 is explicitly discussed in Colpe's critical treatment, also the 1923 essay on the history-of-religions background. It is noteworthy, however, that Colpe never refers to any of the later essays and reviews of Rudolf Bultmann on this topic (see above, nn. 19–22).

this source by the author of the Gospel of John puts this Gospel in a close companionship with such circles and their political as well as religious ambitions. Thus, we must discuss the specifics of the historical situation to which both the source and the Gospel of John belong.

V

Rudolf Bultmann's history-of-religions work is characterized by an impressive thoroughness and comprehensiveness which also includes detailed and careful consideration of philological questions. This is particularly evident in the essay published in two parts in 1928 and 1930 entitled "Investigations in the Gospel of John."[44] The first part studies the term ἀλήθεια (truth), the second part considers the phrase θεὸν οὐδεὶς ἑώρακεν πώποτε ("nobody has ever seen God," John 1:18). In these investigations, it is clear that Bultmann does not isolate the questions of Gnosticism and Gnostic terminology from their larger context. His patient observation of minute detail as well as his grasp of the larger contexts is committed to the whole of Greek philosophy and religion as well as to the Old Testament and Judaism. The clarity in which the relevant materials are presented still calls forth admiration. But one may also ask: What is the price that he had to pay to achieve this clarity?

The first part of this essay, as is well known, became the basis for Bultmann's article "ἀλήθεια" in the *Theologisches Wörterbuch zum Neuen Testament* which was published five years later.[45] It may well have been one of the essays that set the stage for, and determined the structure of, much of the scholarly study contributed to this monumental work. But Bultmann did not, in this essay, follow the typical and often-criticized schema of the articles in the *Theologisches Wörterbuch* which begins with Greek usage, then moves to Hellenism, Old Testament, Judaism, and New Testament. Rather, in his essay of 1928, Bultmann begins with the Old Testament and Judaism, then moves to the New Testament writers whose usage is related to this latter background. After the conclusion of this section, the author discusses the Greek and Hellenistic literature, in which he also includes the *Odes of Solomon* and the *Corpus Hermeticum*, but not Christian writings.

Bultmann's strength in this essay is obvious. He can show the striking difference in the understanding of the term "truth" in the Greek world from Plato to Plotinus as compared to its usage in the Old

[44] "Untersuchungen zum Johannesevangelium," *Exegetica*, 124–97.
[45] Ed. Gerhard Kittel, vol. 1 (Stuttgart: Kohlhammer, 1933) 239–51.

Testament and in the literature of Judaism. The New Testament's use of the term appears as a continuation of the Old Testament concept, and other Christian authors are missing altogether. The Alexandrian theologians Clement and Origen do not appear (although Plotinus is discussed), and Philo of Alexandria is treated as part of the chapter on Hellenism. This one-sided but fascinating and richly documented presentation of a topic in its Greek understanding is equally evident in Bultmann's essay on the history of the symbolism of light in antiquity.[46] The essay begins with an extensive treatment of the classical Greek tragedies, Pindar, and Hesiod, discusses Plato and Aristotle, presents the striking changes which took place in the Hellenistic period (the Stoics, Philo, and the mystery religions are mentioned), and concludes with Plotinus. But no lines are drawn to the Christian literature of the period, nor does the author consider how Christian usage may have influenced the mystery religions and Plotinus. But it remains somewhat ambiguous where the Christian writings really belong in this context. The evidence is divided along some traditional lines which do not quite reflect the actual historical relationships. In terms of word study, this may be justified; however, it is no longer possible to see the interaction between Jewish, Hellenistic, and Christian concepts in the understanding of existence in a particular historical moment as it is reflected in such terminology.

Analogous questions could be asked with respect to the last of these history-of-religions essays, Bultmann's response to the book of Ernst Percy on the origin of Johannine theology.[47] Bultmann criticizes Percy's statements about certain terms which simply fix these terms in a general theoretical system, and he rejects the abstract differentiations of details of a concept. He requests that the interpreter should not be satisfied with the claim that a certain concept agrees with its understanding in a particular "background." Just to say, for example, that the concept "world" in the Gospel of John agrees with the concept of world in the Old Testament does not reveal anything. Rather, the interpreter must explain what it *means* that human beings express the understanding of their own existence through the use of such concepts, "how world is experienced." This emphasis is persistent. Bultmann defines such "meaning" usually in terms of a general phenomenology of religion, that is, the world can be experienced as "hostile," or as "fallen," or as a realm for education. Or Bultmann refers to the

[46] "Zur Geschichte der Lichtsymbolik im Altertum," *Exegetica*, 323–55; see above, n. 21.

[47] "Johanneische Schriften und Gnosis," *Exegetica*, 230–54.

understanding of existence which is expressed in various concepts.[48] But he does not go beyond this interpretation to an explanation of the political and social factors which determine such experience of existence in a particular historical situation.

Moreover, it does not become clear how the Christian authors share with those authors who belong to the "background" of the New Testament the ambiguities and agonies of the understanding of existence in a particular historical moment. The New Testament authors, and by all means Paul and the author of the Gospel of John, remain phenomena sui generis, isolated from the rest. They are shining examples of a true existential, that is, eschatological, understanding of life in faith. In fact, this happens despite Bultmann's better methodological insights, and against his inclination to understand the New Testament as a document of Hellenistic syncretism, and notwithstanding his ability of treating non-Christian documents with unbiased care and considerable empathy.

Nevertheless, the New Testament ultimately appears as a special kind of document—separated from its non-Christian context and isolated from other early Christian literature. This is the consequence of elevating the principle of interpretation, the understanding of existence, into an abstract philosophical principle. Because true eschatological understanding is present only in John and Paul, they cease to be historical phenomena. At this point, Bultmann is a Christian apologist rather than a scholar of the history of religions.

VI

Further work with the Gnostic documents from Nag Hammadi will most likely confirm Bultmann's hypothesis of the existence of a pre-Christian Jewish Gnosticism. Thus, his most controversial hypothesis about the history-of-religions background of the New Testament will be confirmed. But it is our task to treat these documents no longer as "background." To be sure, the hypothesis that the Gnostic movement is a secondary aberration from Christianity still operates with the

[48] With explicit reference to the work of Hans Jonas, *Gnosis und spätantiker Geist*, vol. 1: *Die mythologische Gnosis* (FRLANT 51; Göttingen: Vandenhoeck & Ruprecht, 1934; 2d ed. 1954): "(Percy) reproduces the Gnostic mythology as if it were a kind of dogmatics, instead of interpreting it from the understanding of existence which is expressed in it, although the book of Hans Jonas which he quotes repeatedly offered him the best methodical introduction" (*Exegetica*, 232; cf. 253).

assumption of an original and unique Christian truth, "naturally" developed by John and later perverted by the Gnostics. In this respect, nothing can be added to Bultmann's arguments against Ernst Percy.[49] But our renewed efforts to investigate the relationship between Gnosticism and Christianity must not be limited to the tracing of concepts, mythological metaphors, and religious practices, thus producing much in terms of the detailed observation, however necessary, and little in terms of understanding. Considering both the claim of an original Christian uniqueness and the retreat into the technicalities of so-called objective scholarship, Rudolf Bultmann's work as a history-of-religions scholar offers challenging alternatives.

Some of the principles which Bultmann has accepted from the history-of-religions school and further refined in his work remain important guides for further investigations. Following Bultmann's essay of 1940 in which he defends his work against the criticisms of Ernst Percy, those principles can be summarized as follows:

1) The question of early Christianity's relationship to its religious environment must not be reduced to specific terms and concepts, but must be seen as a problem of the entire language world which Christian and non-Christian authors share.
2) Technical definitions of certain concepts, such as "light" or "world," as more "materialistic" or "religious-ethical" or "spiritual" are meaningless; rather, one must ask for the understanding of human existence which is evident in the use and interpretation of such concepts in specific historical situations.
3) Theological statements about the presence of salvation in Jesus or about the uniqueness of Christianity cannot be used as arguments against the total dependence of Christian soteriological language upon its non-Christian environment. On the contrary—and here Bultmann refers once more to the work of Hans Jonas[50]—the early Christian understanding of Jesus is totally determined by the developed soteriologies of its time, particularly by the soteriology of the Gnostic religion.

It is our task to develop these insights further with respect to their specific historical ramifications. We must learn that early Christianity shares not only the language world of the religions of the late Hellenistic period, but also their agonies, predicaments, and failures. New

[49] "Johanneische Schriften und Gnosis," *Exegetica*, 230–54.
[50] *Exegetica*, 253.

sociological investigations into the religious world of that time will serve to deepen these insights, while games with new literary methods will tend to obscure the critical burden of the task. The important challenge of Christian apologetic theology is obviously more difficult and more frustrating than even Rudolf Bultmann realized.

Dieter Georgi

Rudolf Bultmann's *Theology of the New Testament* Revisited

Rudolf Bultmann's *Theology of the New Testament* has dominated the discussion and the discipline of New Testament theology world-wide since 1948 when the first volume appeared. No other theological book has had a similar and equally lasting impact on friend and foe alike during these almost 40 years. For thousands of theologians it has been much more than a New Testament textbook. It has been their basic systematic theology, their dogmatic, and scores of theology courses have treated Bultmann as if he were a direct colleague of the Barths and the Tillichs. What is the secret of this success? It is the inimitable mix of a critical and a constructive approach. I shall present first the critical, and then the constructive, perspective. Thirdly I shall ask whether this mix is a balanced one, true dialectic as it were, and finally I shall draw some conclusions for us, Bultmann's students and heirs.

The Critical Dimension

Bultmann's concern for a critical theology shows first of all in his consistent emphasis on the historical-critical approach and in his thorough pursuit of its various methods. His *Theology of the New Testament* is influenced by that throughout.

Modern historical-critical studies of the New Testament sharpened their tools first of all in the area of the Jesus question. The first sentence of Bultmann's *Theology* and the most famous sentence of the entire book states: "*The message of Jesus* is a presupposition for the theology of the New Testament rather than a part of that theology itself." This statement proves also that Bultmann belongs to the most radical wing of the life-of-Jesus research, represented by D. F. Strauss. Bultmann's distance to any life-of-Jesus theology, also to that of his students, was the only remaining point of connection with Karl Barth, appreciated also by the latter as Karl Barth told me not so long before he died.

This first sentence of the *Theology* shows the influence of the then newest method of historical criticism, form criticism, of which redaction criticism is but a natural part as Bultmann's *History of the Synoptic Tradition* and Martin Dibelius's *From Tradition to Gospel* prove. It was this form criticism which had shown that the gospels, even the synoptic ones, were documents of faith, and that this applied not merely to the frames of the gospels at large but also to prior arrangements and even to most individual units. The creative milieu of the gospels and of the tradition prior to it was the community created and maintained by the Easter faith and by the possession of the spirit.

Bultmann used form criticism and its twin, tradition criticism, also for the reconstruction of what he called "The Kerygma of the Earliest Church" and "The Kerygma of the Hellenistic Church Aside from Paul." Inseparably united with form and tradition criticism is the search for the "Sitz im Leben." Inquiries into it are behind Bultmann's paragraphs on "The Earliest Church as the Eschatological Congregation," on "Beginnings toward Development of Ecclesiastical Forms," on "Church Consciousness and the Christian's Relation to the World," and it shows to a degree also in the paragraphs on "The Sacraments," and on "The Spirit." In the second volume the question of the "Sitz im Leben" is most of all behind chapter 5, "The Rise of Church Order and Its Earliest Development."

The *History of the Synoptic Tradition*, and even more the commentaries on the Gospel of John and on the Johannine Epistles, associate Bultmann for everyone with source criticism which in our student days was still part of what used to be called "Literarkritik," quite different from literary criticism, so much in vogue today. Thus "The Theology of the Gospel of John and the Johannine Epistles" presupposes (as much as the discussion of the Synoptic Gospels) source criticism. But source criticism as "Literarkritik" deals also with matters of integrity and authenticity of our present documents and of whatever source may be behind them. This shows in Bultmann's treatment of Paul and the pseudonymous Pauline epistles and deals with them separately. The latter ones Bultmann discusses only in the latter part of the second volume. Thus this separation reaches deep into the description of the history of the early catholic church. In this, as in many other issues still to be touched upon, Bultmann is a faithful student of F. C. Baur.

But Bultmann is most of all a student of the *Religionsgeschichtliche Schule*, thus committed to the religio-historical method. The impact of Hermann Gunkel's famous study *Die Wirkungen des Heiligen Geistes nach der populären Anschauung der apostolischen Zeit und der Lehre des Apostels Paulus* shows many a time, most of all in Bultmann's discussion of the sacraments and of the spirit, and so do the works of other "Religionsgeschichtler," especially R. Reitzenstein's. The Near East and even more the Hellenistic form of the Mediterranean presented the history-of-religions scholars with dialogical cultures. The history-of-religions school wanted to understand this dialogue, usually listed under syncretism. Biblical religion was rightly seen as a many-phased experience in syncretism. The history-of-religions school's interest in apocalypticism is not followed by Bultmann. Bultmann shares more their interest in Hellenism, and most of all in Gnosticism. Here Bultmann contributes much of his own original religio-historical research. This is demonstrated in the paragraph "Gnostic Motifs" but is found elsewhere, too, many a time. Although not much recognized by today's New Testament scholars who tend to appreciate socio-historical inquiry only if it is dressed in fashionable sociologese, the history-of-religions school had definite socio-historical interests. It certainly was somewhat romantic as the concept of "Volksreligion" demonstrated. The concern of form and tradition criticism for the expression of nonliterary people shows in Bultmann's discussion of the theology of the early church. The interest in the "Sitze im Leben" has been mentioned already. "Primitive phenomena" like sacramentalism and mass phenomena like the Gnostic movement play a heavy role in Bultmann's historical and theological deliberations.

This brings me to the next aspect of critical inquiry, an aspect with which Bultmann has become most of all identified, for better or for worse, that of theological criticism. His teachers of the history-of-religions school made him most of all aware of the range and importance of the myths, not just in the environment of the Old and New Testament or merely in apocrypha and pseudepigrapha but heavily in the Bible itself, not the least in the New Testament. In a way, Bultmann takes the mythological material in the New Testament more seriously than his teachers when he makes his famous demand of demythologizing the New Testament. He understands the syllable *de-* in demythologizing not as stripping the New Testament of things mythical but as reinterpreting the mythical elements and aspects which are not in the periphery of New Testament theology alone but in the very center, in christology and eschatology. Thus demythologizing for Bultmann is an essential part of his hermeneutical program. Hermeneutics in Bultmann's intent is a critical discipline, too. Understanding is not without translation. But translation is not without honest awareness of the character and degree of difference and distance. Thus critical assessment of the foreignness of the New Testament and of its world is an essential part of his hermeneutical approach.

Bultmann's theological criticism does not merely show in his hermeneutics. In the succession of Martin Luther, Bultmann exercises what the Germans call *Sachkritik* which for the main part can be interpreted as canon criticism. It is intimately related to the other critical ventures mentioned. They have sharpened Bultmann's awareness of plurality, particularly of the plurality of religious phenomena and their expressions. Bultmann opens the reader's eyes also for the wider range of the apocryphal literature. They help him to emphasize certain New Testament colors even more. But they also add different aspects. Thus they often bring to light theological variations of the early church which had been part of its experience but had not left any traces in canonical documents. The chapter on the "Kerygma of the Hellenistic Church" is the best example of that.

These differences discovered within the early church often increase for us the strangeness, if not the absurdity, of Scriptures. But Bultmann takes his readers to see, in such seemingly exotic phenomena, engaging conflicts. He demonstrates that they cannot be properly understood and described by an impartial observer but only by somebody who is taking sides in those reflected conflicts. The exegete is called upon to make judgments, fairly but decidedly.

This requires a renewed definition of center and periphery of the canon, even the denial of theological viability of certain canonical documents and of some of the theological options offered by the New Testament. Bultmann demonstrates the opening up of the canon also by including many extracanonical documents in his deliberations. This does not mean theological relativism; on the contrary, it is part of a definite theological determination.

The Constructive Dimension

A major attraction of Bultmann's *Theology of the New Testament*, especially in the long run, has been the constructive dimension of the book. This shows already in the first constructive element of the book. Bultmann presupposes the Easter faith as basis of the Christian experience and community, not the Jesus-experience prior to Easter. Bultmann thus belongs squarely in the camp of the D. F. Strauss of 1835. Strauss had put Easter faith at the heart of the new community. He had shown the importance of the mythologizing character of that faith. It was not privatistic but communal, that is, *collective consciousness*. In Bultmann's *Theology* more than half of the work deals with collective phenomena, not just the earliest and the Hellenistic church, but later on also the growing ancient church.

In his *Theology* Bultmann does not use the pointed formulation made elsewhere that Jesus is risen into the kerygma of the early church, but his outline and discussion present something like that de facto. The eschatological experience of the early church Bultmann sees described most of all in christological terms centered in the experience of the presence of Jesus as eschatological functionary communicated by the kerygma. Bultmann's critical reconstruction portrays the kerygma as the continuous call for authentic existence, and he describes the growing theologies of the early church as responses to the call expressed in theological sketches which reflect the various dialogues between proclamation and authentic self-understanding.

In order to understand that properly, discussion and critical reconstruction of the historical contexts are essential for Bultmann. These contexts are namely responsible for the particular profiles of these theological sketches. The differences are more than products of psychological conditions, individual temperaments or preferences. In Bultmann's opinion, different religious environments, their problems, questions, and offerings, are responsible for the differences between the various segments of the early church and their theologies. They explain in particular the differences between Paul and John.

But there is also another, deeper reason why for Bultmann the recognition of the historical condition is essential. It deals with pre-understanding, and pre-understanding is also an understanding of the human condition at large, that is, of anthropology. Thus for Bultmann anthropology is the secret theme of theology. Paul is so important for Bultmann because he—according to Bultmann—has been most conscious of anthropology as a theological theme, and he has organized his theological reflection around it, most of all in the epistle to the Romans. Thus this letter provides the outline for Bultmann's discussion of the theology of Paul.

But still, Bultmann remains conscious of the fact that eschatology was extremely important for the early church's christology and ecclesiology which—in Bultmann's eyes—were but functions of eschatology. Thus, in Bultmann's presentation of the theologies of the early church, "eschatological" becomes the key term. It describes for Bultmann the dialectic between "final" and "anew," a dialectic characteristic for the proclamation of the Kerygma as well as for faith's responding. "Eschatological" relates evenly to the existential and to the historical. Bultmann loves to describe it with the Pauline ὡς μή, the paradox of the "not yet—already."

Given this dialectical balance the concept of the "eschatological" according to Bultmann protects theology against legalism, christology against mythology (or rather, ideology), ecclesiology against soteriological engineering; the concept of the "eschatological" shields ethics against activism and quietism. Eschatological existence is authentic existence. It expresses itself in trustful obedience, justified by this faith alone, equally distant from boastfulness and self-damnation, enthusiasm and institutionalism.

Is there a Balance between the Critical and the Constructive?

How concrete, how real, how communal can this dialectic become? Here the reader of Bultmann's *Theology* notices an interesting disparity. Theoretically, it centers on the Easter faith of the early church, that is, on a communal phenomenon. But, in fact, Bultmann constantly directs the reader's attention to individuals. This starts already with the presentation of Jesus. Jesus' proclamation receives as much space as the theologies of the early church aside from Paul, that is, the communities first expressing the Easter faith.

Even more attention is given to the anonymous author of the Gospel of John. But the relatively largest portion of the entire book is devoted to Paul, almost a third of the *Theology.* This is not merely due to the quantitative reason that Paul, authentic as well as pseudonymous, represents such a large part of the canon. This preference has, most of all, qualitative reasons. Bultmann thinks heavily in terms of self, individual, and therefore also of individual authorship. The *work* of a certain author, his achievement, his originality, deserves special attention. It is amazing how often the concept originality appears. Already in the *History of the Synoptic Tradition* the yardstick of originality had been used as decisive criterion in determining authenticity or inauthenticity of Jesus' words. There "authentic," "original," and "eschatological" are very close.

This shift from the communal to the individual is found throughout Bultmann's *Theology.* In his epilogue Bultmann says that the task of a theology of New Testament is "to interpret the theological thoughts of the New Testament in their connection with the 'act of living.'" But this "act of living" (a term adopted from Adolf Schlatter) then is defined as "believing self-understanding." Given the preceding discussion in the book, "believing self-understanding" means the new understanding of the self in concrete historical encounter being called upon to trust and to decide. But this abstract talk and this decisionalism empty the very living, its peculiarities as much as its communal dimensions. The almost complete silence of the *Theology* with respect to the details of situation of New Testament writers and audiences, particularly as to contextual problems and responses, is also a matter of principle. Bultmann's horror of legalism, his insistence on transcendence in the encounter between proclamation and existence call for the abstract, for the private. They do not allow any described concreteness.

Bultmann says at the same place in his *Theology* that theological meaning is not to be seen "as theological teachings, timeless general truths." But in the work preceding the epilogue Bultmann had led the reader from one term to the next, from concept to concept, particularly in the central part, the discussion of the theologies of Paul and of John.

Bultmann's closeness to F. C. Baur and to D. F. Strauss might have tempted the reader to understand this preference for concepts in a Hegelian sense, that is, concepts as expressions of consciousness, not just individual but also collective. But the term "consciousness" is avoided by Bultmann. It is replaced by self-understanding, even in collective references. Bultmann actually polemicizes against the use of the term "consciousness" which he individualizes and psychologizes. Bultmann leaves out the collective and epochal meaning of the term so influential since Hegel.

Therefore, Bultmann's closeness to F. C. Baur with respect to the importance of conflicts in the early church, radicalized by Walter Bauer's *Orthodoxy and Heresy in Earliest Christianity*, does not lead to much. Neither the Judaizers nor the Christian Gnostics receive much treatment in Bultmann's *Theology*. They remain shadows at best—despite the fact that they represent the majority in the church of the first and second century.

Although Bultmann in his paragraph on the development towards the Christian canon shows the appropriate liberal disdain for the canon, de facto he sides with the winners and against the losers. Bultmann's decision is, not to critically reconstruct the early church's dialogues and conflicts within and without, but to interpret the documents of the New Testament—and that is still most of all the canon—to the present day. Therefore, Bultmann's endeavor is heavily apologetic.

The theological claim of that approach is that the New Testament, or better its core, Paul and John, reflect revelation, not one among many, but *the* revelation, *the* new self-understanding. And then there is the not-so-hidden claim, that this is historically verifiable, that this newness can be demonstrated in comparison with other religious offerings of the time, most of all Judaism and Gnosticism. In fact, Bultmann puts the proof of historical uniqueness of the core of the canon side by side with the claim of revelation. Revelation is proven by way of demonstrating historical superiority in which canonical survival is an argument and factor.

The history-of-religions school had not been fascinated with the immense variety of religious options in and around the early church alone. The attempt to respect the integrity of these options perturbed the minds of these scholars. They had grown up with the assumption of their Christian environment that the revealed religion (and Christian civilization) possessed a natural and self-evident superiority over other religious phenomena, and this was supposed to be taught in the theological curriculum. Ernst Troeltsch, the systematic theologian of the history-of-religions school, expresses this perturbance in his *On the Absoluteness of Christianity.* There is nothing of that perturbance in Rudolf Bultmann. He opposes what he calls the relativism of the history-of-religions school. Again I need to mention the term "eschatological." It works for Bultmann and for many New Testament scholars and systematic theologians ever since as a magic wand. Whereas for the history-of-religions school the term "eschatological" described the foreignness of Jesus and of the early church—together with Jewish apocalypticism and other comparable ancient eschatologies—for Bultmann and many contemporary New Testament scholars and Christian theologians the term "eschatological" stands for the novelty of Christianity, its incomparable superiority, the uniqueness of the victorious religion, deservedly victorious. Wherever a comparison is ventured, wherever analogies lift their head, wherever challenges are heard from other religious options but the canonical ones, the invocation of the "eschatological" is made, and the demons, the shadows have to disappear. Historical criticism thus turns into exorcism.

Thus my major criticism of Bultmann's *Theology* is that it demonstrates an inability to keep criticism and construction in continuous dialectical relationship. Especially the historical dimension of Bultmann's criticism is cut short. This does not merely apply to the historical context of the New Testament and of its documents, it applies also to the historical context of the theologian Rudolf Bultmann. He presents the constructive side of his *Theology* as *interpretation* of the New Testament message to the modern reader. But does he really address the reader in his or her context? Is that context of any importance for him as historian and theologian? In his book on Bultmann, Walter Schmithals quotes a significant passage from a letter

Bultmann wrote in 1926 to an engaged theologian from Frankfurt/ Main, E. Foerster:

> Of course, the impact of the war has led many people to revise their concepts of human existence; but I confess that that has not been so in my case. Perhaps I am again going too far towards the other extreme, but I must be frank; the war was not a shattering experience for me. Of course there were a great many individual things, but not the war as such. I am quite clear about this, and I once defended my case in numerous conversations, that war is not so different from peace; a shipwreck, an act of meanness, the sort of thing that happens every day, confronts us with exactly the same questions as the heaping up of events in war. So I do not believe that the war has influenced my theology. My view is that if anyone is looking for the genesis of our theology he will find that internal discussion with the theology of our teachers plays an incomparably greater role than the impact of the war or the reading of Dostoievsky.[1]

In 1926, a theologian, particularly one in a historical discipline, should have had enough insight into the makings of World War I not to compare it with catastrophes of nature, mishaps or misdemeanors, war being just a piling up of these. Could one propose doing theology as if nothing had happened? Karl Barth tried that in 1933, but not for long. And Bultmann's own lecture at the start of the summer semester of 1933 speaks for a different attitude than that in 1926. It is to Bultmann's praise that in this lecture he attacked anti-semitic politics of the Nazis at the universities, and unfortunately remained one of the few to protest at that time when protest still could have had an effect. All the more his insight and courage deserve our gratitude. But still, Bultmann took this to be an individual secular venture of his, not directly related to his doing history and theology.

Going back to his statement about his assessment of World War I, Bultmann should have acknowledged the fact that he was a paid officer of the state, a professor, thus an institutional participant in that political and military machine which was involved in the war of 1914–1918, not merely passively but actively. It was a professor's public duty to research, teach, and examine theology. Bultmann should at least have raised one question, namely whether the official theological enterprise he was involved in might not have contributed

[1] Schmithals, *An Introduction to the Theology of Rudolf Bultmann* (Minneapolis: Augsburg, 1968) 9–10.

to the collective, nonsensical crime of the war—a war among allegedly Christian nations. As historical-critical theologian, even more as a critical hermeneuticist, he could not leave out the critical assessment of the condition of his own historical situation. The factual, institutional partiality of the alleged distance and neutrality of the scholar should have been a matter of critical investigation.

Whereas Bultmann states that he was theologically unaffected by World War I, he claims that the critical dialogue with his teachers was cause for the dramatic changes that he among others stands for—usually listed under the rise of form criticism, radical Jesus concept, dialectical theology. How much did he?

I have shown that Bultmann's *Theology* betrays the influence of his teachers, indeed, particularly those of the history-of-religions school. One representative of the history-of-religions school, William Wrede, in 1897 had written a still-exciting essay "Concerning the Task and Method of So-Called New Testament Theology." Bultmann discusses it at some length in the epilogue. But he gives much more attention to Adolf Schlatter than to Wrede, and Schlatter holds the rung of the ladder next to Bultmann. Is Bultmann's *Theology* thus more Schlatter than Wrede? Not quite. The role of Jesus, of Hellenism and of Gnosticism, the understanding of δικαιοσύνη and of John, and many more features would speak against such an identification. But the discovered apologetic bias belongs in the vein of Schlatter.

Bultmann's *Theology* shows that his dialogue with his teachers of the history-of-religions school had not been intensive enough. He had cut short the *theological* challenge of their insights regarding historical distance, religious pluralism, common religion, syncretism, historical process, interplay of form and content, and social context. And he had not developed the same interest in *political* engagement, not just of the individual scholar alone but also of scholarship at large. The history-of-religions school expressed its collective political interest among others in publishing ventures like "Die Schriften des Alten und des Neuen Testaments," the "Religionsgeschichtliche Volksbücher," first-hand critical scholarly research in books for the general public. And the monumental encyclopedic enterprise of the history-of-religions school, the first edition of *Die Religion in Geschichte und Gegenwart*, stood at the threshold between scholarship and the public. All of this demonstrates the closeness of the history-of-religions school to the politically rather important international adult-education movement. The one who had demonstrated this involvement most drastically had been Ernst Troeltsch, who much to the chagrin of his academic colleagues at Berlin, after the revolution had become in 1919 part-time undersecretary of state for Protestant affairs in the ministry of culture of the State of Prussia, an anti-monarchical government under a social-democratic prime-minister. This public engagement of Ernst Troeltsch was not unrelated to his publications.

We, the heirs of Rudolf Bultmann, stand with him in that tradition of the history-of-religions school, and we have to complete their task as historical theologians which most of them were prevented from doing by premature death: Bousset at 55 years, Heitmüller at 56, Troeltsch at 57, Weiss at 50, and Wrede at 47.

Some Suggestions

New Testament theology is first of all a historical discipline. It finds Paul and many more Jesus-believers as Jews and sees them take the LXX as their Bible. Therefore, Wrede's request needs to be heeded that a New Testament theology has to evolve out of a description of the Jewish "mother-soil of Christianity," particularly out of the discussion of Jewish religion and theology. This provides also the possibility of a new look at a *biblical* theology rather different from the ahistorical and acritical ventures in that area today.

Wrede firmly states that the discussion of pagan Hellenistic phenomena would have to come second as description of the environment Christianity moved towards. More recent research has shown that Judaism of New Testament times was an even more diversified phenomenon than the history-of-religions school had correctly held against Strack, Schürer, Schlatter, and Moore. The dialogue of Judaism with Hellenism at large now is taken more seriously. The Nag Hammadi documents have finally proven that even much of Gnosticism is of Jewish origin. Bultmann's attempt to use Judaism as dark monochrome foil in order to portray Christianity as a bright new star was proven wrong already by the research of the history-of-religions school. All the firsts credited to the inventiveness of Jesus-believers, thus justifying calling Christianity a *new* religion, a revelatory phenomenon in fact, are no firsts at all; for example, universality, pluralism, liberality, a- and anti-nomianism, radical eschatology, even the interpretation of certain historical individuals as eschatological agents and as hermeneutical focus and center for communal belief can all be found in the Judaism of New Testament times, and much of it can be observed in paganism, too.

Why should a Jesus-oriented theology, why should a theology of the New Testament, actually concentrate on the claim of uniqueness—a counterfeit in fact? Why should the theology of the New Testament not pursue the question, historically appropriate and theologically certainly relevant, in what way the Jesus-oriented groups can be seen and understood as representative for Judaism of the first century?

This leads to the next question, which is based on the fact that as to religious phenomena of the Mediterranean, Judaism, including the Jesus groups, provides us with the largest amount of data about that time relative to our information about other religious phenomena which had existed at that time. The assumption of Judaism as a ghetto phenomenon can be proven wrong. We can pursue the historically as well as theologically important question, how much Judaism—Jesus-believers included—can be seen as symptomatic and representative for Hellenism at large, particularly for the religious world of the first century, including the tendency of certain Jewish believers and groups toward elitism and isolationism.

Bultmann never raises the very important historical and theological question whether people like Apollonius of Tyana, Paul and Hillel had not more in common with each other than with us? Neither the Judaism nor the Christianity we know existed during the first century anyhow. This shows the degree of foreignness a theology of the New Testament has to confront.

Wrede is correct in stressing the historical dimension of New Testament theology more than Bultmann does. But Wrede still isolates religion too much from its social and cultural environments.

Religions in general, and the various versions of Judaism in particular, were part of the social organization of the Mediterranean. Already the large quantity of parenetical material in early Christian literature proves that Jesus-believers possessed interest in social organization also. Many cherished theological themes like δικαιοσύνη, χάρις, πίστις, and σῶμα contain social messages, too. Much of the religious world of the first century—including Roman political theology—provides us with attempts and models of social experimentation in a time of extreme changes, with revolution from above as well as from below among them. Many of these religious experiments, certainly those in Judaism, particularly among the Jesus groups, can be seen best as experiments in strategies of social consent. Some were more conservative, some reformist, but there were also rebellious and revolutionary ones among them. Myth in particular proved to be a major instrument in the strategies of social consent.

A theology of the New Testament has to deal with the contributions Jesus-believers made to this world-wide experimentation with strategies of social consent. This experimentation was not so much a matter of great individuals but it depended on collective experience and it was measured by the degree of collective realization. Therefore, the term "consciousness" in a Hegelian sense is more helpful than the term "self-understanding."

As a theology of the New Testament elaborates on the commonality of individual New Testament theologies with experiments of its own time and on the foreignness of these phenomena with respect to us, some rather explosive theological questions raise their head:

1) Is not the task of a critical theology, especially one of the New Testament and of the Bible at large, to uncover the suppressive manipulation a so-called Christian culture, and in particular Christian power structures, have exercised on the tradition which has become ours?
2) Is it not our task to uncover the foreignness of our sources, their difference from us, and their integrity over against us, and are we not to do this as a challenge to a history of interpretation and of application which heavily was and is a history of suppression under which also scores of people have had to suffer and still do so today?
3) And could it not be that a strictly historical-critical theology of the New Testament might not raise anew the scepter of commonality and solidarity as *the* theological *proprium* instead of Christian uniqueness which is at the core of white male Christian imperialism?

Let me finish with quoting part of the most political text of the New Testament (Phil 2:6–11):

> (Χριστὸς Ἰησοῦς) . . . ἑαυτὸν ἐκένωσεν
> . . . ἐν ὁμοιώματι ἀνθρώπων γενόμενος
> . . . ἐταπείνωσεν ἑαυτὸν
> γενόμενος ὑπήκοος μέχρι θανάτου . . .
> διὸ καὶ ὁ θεὸς αὐτὸν ὑπερύψωσεν
> καὶ ἐχαρίσατο αὐτῷ τὸ ὄνομα τὸ ὑπὲρ πᾶν ὄνομα
> ἵνα ἐν τῷ ὀνόματι Ἰησοῦ πᾶν γόνυ κάμψῃ . . .
> καὶ πᾶσα γλῶσσα ἐξομολογήσηται
> ὅτι κύριος Ἰησοῦς Χριστός. . . .

The Englishing of Bultmann: Louise Pettibone Smith

Louise Pettibone Smith, Rudolf Bultmann, and Wellesley

Paul Lehmann

Colleagues Remember Louise

Lucetta Mowry
Harvey McArthur

Students Remember Miss Smith

Mary Martin MacRae
Alice Elder Leake
Priscilla Ham Alexander
Pearl Kosby Russo

Paul Lehmann

Louise Pettibone Smith, Rudolf Bultmann, and Wellesley

In the Introduction to the English translation of the first volume of Rudolf Bultmann's *Glauben und Verstehen*, Robert Funk notes that "very little of Bultmann's work had been translated into English at the time the Second World War broke out."[1] To this comment, he adds the following footnote:

> One notable exception is Louise Pettibone Smith's translation (with E. H. Lantero) from the German *Jesus* (Berlin: Deutsche Bibliothek, 1926; 2/1929) as *Jesus and the Word* (New York, Scribner, 1934; paperback edition, 1953). Unlike the vast majority of such cases, the alteration in the title in this instance was an illuminating advance over the German form. Professor Smith remarked in her Preface to the paperback edition that Bultmann was little known in the United States in 1934. It is altogether fitting that she, who led the way in presenting Bultmann originally to English readers, should return after so many years to the unfinished task of providing the wider context for *Jesus and the Word*.[2]

Accordingly, it is also "altogether fitting," that a centenary commemorative Symposium honoring the birth, life, and work of Rudolf Bultmann should include in its consideration a tribute of respect and admiration, of remembrance and gratitude for the life and work of Louise Pettibone Smith. That Louise Smith should have provided Bultmann with an English title marking an "illuminating advance over the German form," succinctly and simply identifies who she was and is, what she was about, and how she went about it. On Bultmann's

[1] *Faith and Understanding*, vol. 1 (ed. Robert W. Funk; trans. Louise Pettibone Smith; New York and Evanston: Harper & Row, 1969) 10.

[2] Ibid., 10 n. 2.

behalf, she broke down the "middle wall of partition" (Eph 2:14), dividing the monolingual Anglo-Saxons from their multilingual fellow "travellers through time as they bumble by from birth to death menaced by madness."[3]

Louise Smith was not only a translator of Bultmann. She was also his travel agent in the United States. Consequently, Wellesley College became a kind of center of Bultmannian operations, "not only in Judea and Samaria," in their American counterparts, but "in the uttermost parts of the earth" (Acts 1:8b). As I shall venture to suggest in what follows, the breaking down of the middle wall of partition became for Louise, and for many of us with her, in the power of the "chief cornerstone" (Eph 2:20), a bulwark against the time when Bonzo should emerge from Death Valley, and emerge only long enough to leave no stone unturned until all dissenters should be buried there, beyond any prospect of the resurrection of the dead. Thus, when such a Symposium convenes at Wellesley College, to the Faculty of which belonged this distinguished and stalwart Biblical scholar, who happened also to be an Anglo-Saxon of formidable Yankee and Calvinist chromosomes and convictions, it is simply providential wisdom, decency and order—and in that order—that Louise Pettibone Smith should be present to us and with us.

In her youth, Louise had learned the difference between Babel and Pentecost; and she was, though she would cringe at the thought, a Pentecostalist from beginning to end. As far as the heavens are from the earth, so far—it has turned out—is a Pentecostalist in Wellesley from a Pentecostalist Presbyterian in Dallas, who imagines that the second Great Awakening in January 1985 can make Death Valley blossom as a rose.

Louise Pettibone Smith was a professor of Biblical History, Literature and Interpretation at Wellesley from 1915 onwards, and until her retirement in 1953. In those days, the *Nephilim* were in this place; and the *Rephaim* too: that is, the fallen ones and the fearsome ones (Gen 6:4; Num 13:33). But in those days, the seed of Abraham and Sarah had not yet been outvoted by the pluralistic, synergistic, syncretistic fascinations with the *Baalim*, by the Canaanites who were and still are in the land; and who continue to pursue the fantasy that Babel *is* Pentecost. I believe they call it "Religion." In any event, to a young and inexperienced colleague, as ignorant as he was innocent, both of the *Nephilim* and of the *Rephaim*, Louise Smith was in truth "among those who were encountered as giants" (Deut 2:11, 20).

[3] W. H. Auden, *The Age of Anxiety* (New York: Random House, 1947) 23.

It is neither accidental nor coincidental that Louise's *Alma Mater*, Bryn Mawr, should have included her among the seventy-five distinguished alumnae to be awarded honorary doctorates upon the occasion of the college's seventy-fifth anniversary. Indeed, among Louise's impressive gifts were a single-minded dedication to scholarship and learning as a fulfilling vocation, to teaching with imagination, precision and conviction, and to a passion and compassion for the "stranger within the gate" (Deut 5:14; 10:18–19; 26:13); that is, for the outsiders and those to whom the insiders responded with the disregard of alienation and by the subtle and not so subtle preferences of power, so structured as to deny to the different, a meaningful participation in human community.

Let me, then, invite our respect and admiration, remembrance and gratitude for these gifts; and this, more briefly than is their due, and much more inadequately than they require. As an *aide-mémoire*, let us, in the tradition of Rudolf Bultmann, engage in what he called *Sachkritik*. This *Sachkritik* has to do with *The Word and the Words*, implied in Louise's imaginative title. *The Word and the Words* in the encounter with her gifts, offers the hope that in remembrance and gratitude, Louise Pettibone Smith may come among us again.

When I think of Louise's dedication to scholarship and learning as a vocation, the identifying word that comes to mind is "conscientiousness." When I recall her teaching with imagination and precision, the word "conviction" claims attention. And when the surprise of her retirement activity overtakes my meeting again with her on this occasion, it is the word "conscience" that makes her passion and compassion for the stranger within the gate understandable and unavoidable. Each of these indications of the point and purpose and ethos of her life becomes, when taken together, an invitation to each of us—in welcoming her among us again—to bring commitment and responsibility together, as the point and purpose and ethos of the living of our days.

It was Louise's formidable scholarship and exacting learning that compounded her considerable stature by nature with a yet more considerable stature by grace. She was, indeed, among the giants of the faculty at Wellesley, and in the department of Biblical History, Literature and Interpretation, in the days when I first came to know her here in 1941. There were *Rephaim* and *Nephilim* in the land: the fearsome ones and the fallen ones. Had I known, or could I even have guessed that this moving privilege would be mine this evening, I would certainly have tried her patience with my vincible ignorance, by asking her to explain to me the subtleties of Hebrew vocabulary, syntax and folk-lore, having to do with the *Rephaim* and the *Nephilim*. Having failed to do so, I can only commend my lack of foresight—and even curiosity—to the forbearance of my colleagues in Semitic and Old Testament Studies in this notable gathering; and, in my extremity, venture upon a semantic suspicion of my own, quickened by Louise Pettibone Smith. She had a way of evoking such suspicions, not only in her students, but in her colleagues as well.

My Smithian suspicion is that the difference between the *Rephaim* and the *Nephilim* is a not insignificant one. There are those in whom commitment and responsibility are so *con*joined in competence and excellence as "to fill the mind with never ending wonder and awe," as Kant once said about the stars. These are the fearsome ones, the *Rephaim.* On the other hand, there are those in whom commitment and responsibility are so *dis*joined as to center commitment upon themselves and to cultivate responsibility as the sign and measure of self-justifying self-esteem. These are the fallen ones, the *Nephilim.* And they are busy again, on campuses and off, at barricading the "naked public square,"[4] even as they fill it with the corpses of the widows and the orphans and the strangers within the gate: victims of the injustice with which, in our time as in other times, the powerful feed their power. In the first instance, commitment and responsibility are sundered by the terrifying dynamics of self-deceived and deceiving destruction, within and without.

At all events, Louise was one of the fearsome ones, whose scholarship and learning were formidable. She pursued them as a commitment in response to a claim. I used to chide her from time to time for what seemed to me to be her indifference to the world about her. "How can you," I would ask her, "teach the Old Testament, and especially the Prophets, year after year, and never move beyond this campus?" Her unvarying reply was that she had been appointed by the President and the Board of Trustees of Wellesley College to teach in the Department of Biblical History, Literature and Interpretation. And she could only do one thing at a time—"well!" In that "well!" I always heard a silent judgment upon my misguided youthful attempts to be both a scholar and teacher *and* involved in the world. She would have none of it. It took me more than a little while to discover the secret of her conscientiousness.

The secret was the δύναμις (creative power) of her linkage of commitment with responsibility. Perhaps the most notable and memorable sign of her "secret weapon" of conscientiousness was the act of courage expressed in her devotion to Rudolf Bultmann. Her probing of his

[4] Richard Neuhaus, *Naked Public Square* (Grand Rapids: Eerdman's, 1984).

mind and thought involved little short of a *μετάβασις εἰς ἄλλο γένος* ("a radical turning upside down") of the path of scholarship and learning which led her to Bultmann and became the path which she was to continue to pursue. To start all over again—*that*, I submit, is courage!

In Louise, this *conscientiousness* was companioned by a rare combination of imagination and precision, through her being about whatever she was about, with *conviction.* At this point, the paradoxical identity of Louise Pettibone Smith shows itself in a particularly impressive way. By many of her colleagues and students, she was at once respected and ignored, even disliked. The diffidence that companioned her resoluteness was not readily discernible. As a Yankee and a Calvinist, she found it so impossible to wear her heart on her sleeve as to suggest that coldness of heart was her hidden *élan*. I have found myself speculating about this more than once, during the intervening years. And especially, as I have thought about our coming together here, a number of biographical footnotes in illumination of this point have occurred to me.

As I have said, Louise was nurtured as a Yankee and a Calvinist. She used to tell me about her puzzlement as a child over her grandfather. This awesome gentleman never seemed to communicate—not only *not* with children, but not even with adults. As she grew older and wiser, it occurred to her one day, that the secret of her grandfather's inability to communicate was his clear and certain knowledge of the providential grace of God. It seems that, especially on holidays, her immediate family would join with other members of the clan at Grandfather's House and Board. At the festive table Grandfather, to whom nobody would dream of talking unless addressed by him, and from whom nobody would expect to hear very much, used to pray upwards of fifteen to twenty minutes before the ample and tempting meal could be partaken of. Eventually, it dawned upon Louise that her Grandfather was not only giving thanks to God as the Giver of all good. He was expressing before God all his deepest feelings and concerns for those whom he loved most, and which he was unable to express to them face to face.

Or there was Uncle Ben, who loved strawberries to the point of an addiction. Every year at strawberry season, the family would gather about Uncle Ben's table upon which he would ceremonially set down a huge bowl of strawberries and firmly announce: "Doubtless, God could have made a better berry; but obviously, God did *not* make a better berry!" The reticence and unaffected pleasure nurtured in her family, Louise brought with her to Wellesley where they found expression through an acute and carefully considered *conviction*.

An incidental instance concerns another of my chidings of Louise. She took particular pleasure in attending worship on Sunday when the sacrament of Baptism was being celebrated. I used to tell her that these services were most diverting and frustrating to me because the infants were always screaming so that one couldn't pay attention to the Word and the words. To this caveat, Louise's reply was: "The screaming of infants at Baptism is always especially meaningful to me because it is a proper protest of nature against grace."

Two further cases in point may be noted in relation to a student event to which the college community looked forward each year and to an administrative procedure internal to the Department of Biblical History during her tenure as its Chairperson. At Wellesley the Junior Class produces and presents each year what is known as "The Junior Show." This spectacle centered upon one or another member of the faculty, and came to be regarded as a distinction of favor conferred by the students upon the faculty member chosen as the subject of the evening's frivolity. One year during my time here the choice fell upon Louise. One of the directives most urged upon her was to express her exasperation at whatever it was that was going on, through a punch line that seemed to the Juniors to be vintage Louise Pettibone Smith. They wanted her to exclaim in chagrin, "Oh, for heaven's sake!" As for a possible alternative like "Oh, for God's sake!" the producers and Louise were unanimous in the conviction that *that* would not do. And as for the proposed line, Louise resolutely refused. "I will only say what I was brought up to say in such situations," she explained. She finally prevailed; and the line turned out to be, "Shucks and peanut shells!" The line brought down the house, contrary to all directional forebodence; and it made her the star of the show. It was indeed vintage Louise.

As for the biblical department, it happened that during my first year as a member of the faculty, I was appointed to serve on the administrative committee. I was reluctant to accept the appointment because of a conviction of my own which was that the better part of wisdom for newcomers in a faculty was to keep eyes and ears open and mouth shut, at least for the first year. One did not, however, refuse Louise Smith on a matter of departmental responsibility, even when she was not the Chairperson. So I reluctantly agreed. Early in the Autumn of 1941, the agenda before the "Small Committee," as it was called, included an item having to do with an appointment to the faculty of the department. On the basis of my brief acquaintance with the candidate under consideration and of the discussion of my colleagues, it seemed to me appropriate to abstain when the vote was called for. It did not seem so to Louise. Apparently, there had recently been a colleague who, as a member of the Committee, seemed unable or unwilling to come to a decision and always abstained. Let her identity be cared for by the sign of "X." Upon my abstention, Louise turned directly to me and, with unmistakable impatience and annoyance, emphatically declared: "We won't have any more X's in this department! You vote!" So I did vote, and as a lone minority of one, against the resolution to appoint. It was not the decision which Louise found irresponsible, even though it did not agree with hers. It was indecisiveness which she found inadmissible and inexcusable. Thus did *conscientiousness* combine with *conviction* about who she was and why. The combination spelled integrity to which one could only respond with respect and admiration.

In view of Louise's somewhat aloof disposition, respect for those with whom she disagreed was as remarkable as it was recognizable. But there was one notable precondition. She had great respect for those with whom she disagreed, in whom could be discerned a kindred discipline of scholarship and teaching with imagination, precision, and conviction. We come here upon the basic paradox of her conscientiousness and conviction. This was the conviction that the discipline of responsibility is the gift and practice of freedom. The nexus of this formative paradox is, and was for her, the unashamed acknowledgment and acceptance of the claims of *conscience.*

A notable, even historic, instance of Louise's conscience in action is provided by the surprise of her activities preceding and following upon her retirement.

In the difficult days of the early fifties, to the lasting credit of Wellesley (and perhaps also of Harvard), there were only two professors in the colleges of New England who were summoned before the Senate Internal Security Sub-Committee, headed by Senator Jenner. One of them was Kirtley Mather, a renowned Geologist at Harvard; the other was Louise Pettibone Smith of Wellesley. The Sub-Committee was meeting in Boston, before which Louise was summoned to appear on March 26, 1953. Her testimony has always seemed to me to be an act of courage in conscience, companioning the act of courage in conscientiousness and conviction in her discovery and commitment to Rudolf Bultmann. It must also be gratefully acknowledged that, to the great credit of the Board of Trustees of this College, Louise was assured of the Board's readiness to make available to her its support and such legal assistance as she might have need of in connection with her appearance before the Sub-Committee.

The interrogation went something like this:

> "You are Louise Pettibone Smith?"
>
> "Yes."
>
> "You are a Professor of Wellesley College?"
>
> "I was," said Louise; "I am about to retire."
>
> "We have here a note which says you know a certain Mr. Patterson." (Patterson was then a prime target of the Sub-Committee, accused of being a member of the Communist Party.)
>
> "I have debated with Mr. Patterson a number of times," Louise said. "But I do not know him."
>
> "Did you know that he was a member of the Communist Party of the United States?"
>
> "No," said Louise. "I have heard it told that he was, but I don't know it."
>
> "If you did know it, would it make any difference?"
>
> "No," said Louise. "I am sixty-five years of age and have been following my own judgment these many years; and I think I trust my judgment more than Tom Clark's." (Thomas C. Clark was the recent Attorney-General of the United States who had prepared the infamous list of subversive organizations.)
>
> "Witness dismissed."

Well, in the light of my earlier chidings of Louise's conscience, I was gratified beyond measure. What surprised me still more was that Louise did not let the matter rest there. I had, you see, greatly underestimated the secret power of the integrity which integrated conscientiousness, conviction, and conscience in her being who she was, in what she was about, and how she went about it.

As a Yankee, the rebuke to the Sub-Committee was a natural and self-evident expression of her deeply rooted commitment to the civil liberties, constitutionally safeguarded and indispensable to a democratic society. As a Calvinist, she found it equally natural and self-evident to be aware of and alert to the idolatry of self-righteous self-justification to which all authority and power are vulnerable. In her retirement, these two strains of her heritage were claimed by a providential incongruity for which her teaching of the Bible in this place during all those years had singularly equipped her. She matched her rebuke of one committee by her commitment to the chairing of another. Her rebuke of a committee of overreaching power was followed by the leadership of a committee founded for the sake of human justice, as the foundation and the criterion of the liberties of all people.

Louise accepted the Co-Chair of the American Committee for Protection of Foreign Born in December 1951.[5] This committee had come into existence as far back as 1919, in the wake of the infamous Palmer Raids. These raids exemplified the preference of the United States Department of Justice for terror over due process, and for security over justice, in the alleged protection of the freedom and safety of the body politic. The raids split families, denaturalized and deported citizens suspected of syndicalism and of various other activites informed by a commitment to social justice which Republican Administrations, at least since Theodore Roosevelt and William Howard Taft, have more stubbornly disdained than Democrats, and still do. Between the Palmer Raids and the nomination of Edwin Meese, 3d, as Attorney-General of the United States,[6] the infamous Walter-McCarran Act has presided and prevailed over the slow and subtle erosion of the constitutional guarantees enshrined in the Bill of Rights. It fell to this hitherto little-known Professor of Biblical History, Literature and Interpretation at Wellesley College, both to confound the House Un-American Activities Committee by her testimony which led to the deletion of the American Committee for Protection of Foreign Born from its list of alleged subversive organizations and to write a well-documented history of this Committee entitled, *The Torch of Liberty.*[7]

The principal reason for this retirement commitment, as Louise often explained, was firmly anchored in the Pentateuch; and there, of all places, in the Holiness Code of Leviticus. Therein, it is set down: "You shall have one law for the sojourner and for the native; for I am

[5] On December 9, 1951, the Committee elected Louise Pettibone Smith and George B. Murphy, Jr., as Co-Chairmen, Bishop Arthur Moulton as Honorary Chairman, and Abner Green as Executive Secretary.

[6] A. Mitchell Palmer was President Woodrow Wilson's third Attorney-General in 1919. Edwin Meese, 3d, at the time of this symposium awaits confirmation by the Senate as President Ronald Reagan's Attorney-General. The political kinship between the Palmer Raids and the nomination of Edwin Meese, 3d has been instructively analyzed by Christopher Hitchens, "Minority Report: Why Ed Meese Shouldn't Be Confirmed," in *The Nation*, vol. 239, no. 22, December 29, 1984–January 5, 1985, pp. 697, 701–702.

[7] Louise Pettibone Smith, *The Torch of Liberty* (New York: King, 1959). See esp. Chapter VI, §§ 19–20.

the Lord your God" (Lev 24:22). "When a stranger sojourns in your land you shall not do him wrong. The stranger who sojourns with you shall be to you as the native among you; and you shall love him as yourself; for you were strangers in the land of Egypt: I am the Lord your God" (Lev 19:23–24). Louise was, in truth, among the *Rephaim*, the Hebrew root of which means "to heal."[8]

Biblical scholarship and biblical learning find their moment of conscience. When this moment came upon Louise, she naturally and self-evidently seized it. She went in the power of the Word in the words, across the length and breadth of this land. In groups gathered for meeting, and among individuals, she was listened to, heard, and made welcome by labor leaders and labor rank and file, by immigrants, naturalized citizens and native born, many of whom could not have been more distant on the educational spectrum from the students among whom Louise had lived and worked at Wellesley College. She talked *to* them and *with* them straight from the Pentateuch and from Jeremiah, about the promise, the hope, and the path of a society of justice and freedom and peace, in which there is one law for the sojourner and for the native. She was received everywhere with respect and admiration and gratitude—and with warm hospitality and friendship, in the wonder of the discovery that she, whom they seemed to have known and trusted always, had been a college professor. How fearfully and wonderfully made (Ps 130:14) it is, that on the occasion of the centenary of the founding of the Society of Biblical Literature in 1980, Louise Pettibone Smith should be among the six members of the Society to have been honored by a special citation and that—*Dei providentia*—upon the centenary of the birth of Rudolf Bultmann, this Symposium should remember her in respect and admiration and gratitude.

Our last meeting happened in November of 1980, shortly before she died. All of her capacities of self-discipline and resoluteness, of conscientiousness, conviction, and conscience were then on trial. She had finally to go into the nursing facility of the Retirement Community in Hartford which had become her home. There, she had to share a room with another person whom she simply could not abide. It was, however, vintage Louise, to bear this also, without a murmur. The American Committee for Protection of Foreign Born, to which she had been so ably devoted, had resolved to help make available to her, a

[8] To this surprising confirmation of my Smithian suspicion, my Union Seminary colleague, Professor George Landes, has called my attention, as this tribute was being prepared for publication.

place of her own in the Nursing Facility. But this resolve, too lately made, likewise too lately came to her aid. It succeeded only in transferring her to the waiting list for the next available opening. As we took leave of one another (she was then in her ninety-fourth year) she said, "Paul, one should not live so long." It was an unforgettable sign of her intelligence and her integrity, her diffidence and her forbearance, her faith and her faithfulness that, on the tightrope of faith and doubt, death found her waiting for God's next move.

Louise Pettibone Smith: *Tibi Deum laudamus! Requiescat in pace!*

Colleagues Remember Louise

Lucetta Mowry*

When I first met Louise (during the summer of 1940, I believe, while I was a graduate student at Yale University), I thought that she was one of the "Ladies of the Club"; for she was among the women who had invited me to speak at their church in Winchester, Conn., on the educational work of the missionaries in Korea. When I met her again several years later at Wellesley College, I realized that I had been chatting over a cup of tea with the chairman of the Department of Biblical History, Literature and Interpretation, and that she had not been so much interested in the missionary enterprise as she was in recent developments in biblical research and in neo-orthodoxy. I discovered, too, that she was not a gentle club woman but someone who could shatter what she considered an ill-conceived thought with the speed and skill of a snapping turtle.

Though born in Ogdensburg, New York, she had the blunt, direct frankness of a New England Yankee. Her father had been a newspaper editor in northern New York, and her mother before her marriage had been a teacher as were both of her grandmothers. Since her mother wished to send Louise to what she regarded as the best college for women, Louise went to Bryn Mawr where she majored in Latin and Greek. While teaching English and Latin for three years at Hardin College in Mexico, Missouri, Louise took a correspondence course in Hebrew from the University of Chicago. [This was quite likely with William Rainey Harper, President of the University of Chicago, who continued teaching Hebrew by correspondence for years after he became the founding President at Chicago. —ED.] The study of semitic languages and literature became the central interest in her

*Lucetta Mowry is Professor of Religion and Biblical Studies and Andrew W. Mellon Professor in the Humanities, Emerita, at Wellesley College, where she served on the faculty from 1942 until her retirement in 1978.

professional career, and in her opinion nothing in all that literature compared with the Old Testament prophets and their emphasis on social justice. While working on her doctorate at Bryn Mawr she was selected to be the first woman given a fellowship to study Palestinian archaeology at the American Schools of Oriental Research in Jerusalem. On her trip back to the States she spent the summer of 1914 working at the British Museum on the recently discovered and published Aramaic papyri from Elephantine.

Her pursuit of new trends in theological and historical developments took her to Germany before and after Hitler came to power: first to study at Bonn under Karl Barth and second to learn about the opposition of the German Confessing Church to Hitler. The latter experience convinced her that freedom of information is absolutely essential to freedom of thought and that people are helpless to combat propaganda without factual information. For her consequent activities with Greek refugees in a camp near Gaza and those concerned with civil rights in this country as well as for her scholarly achievements, Bryn Mawr honored her in 1960 with their distinguished service award.

The disciplined and rigorous integrity which characterized Louise's work in biblical studies made an indelible impression on her students and colleagues. The lazy student who came unprepared to her classes quickly learned that a casual, unprofessional attitude toward work was not acceptable; the conscientious student learned that the methods and purpose of biblical research could be applied to other academic disciplines. By organizing monthly department meetings for the discussion of biblical and theological issues and by inviting some of its members to weekly sessions for studying Aramaic and Ugaritic texts, she also trained her colleagues with the expectation that they would share her standards of excellence. For her work as an outstanding teacher it was appropriate that the Society of Biblical Literature on the occasion of its centennial celebration in 1980 recognized her contribution to the academic world by establishing an award bearing her name to honor her leadership and guidance in teaching and to be given periodically to a distinguished teacher. By 1980 Louise had already become a legend in her own lifetime, for the Committee planning this award asked me why, in sending information about her, I had omitted the date of her death. She must have been gratified to know that the effect of her teaching continues to go beyond the limitations of space and time.

Harvey McArthur*

Louise Pettibone Smith was a most unusual person. I came to know her during the academic year 1947–48 when I was teaching in Wellesley's Department of Biblical History. In fact Louise was the one sent in to monitor my teaching and to provide the necessary correction and advice. I think she always suspected that if I had stayed a few years longer at Wellesley they could have made a good teacher out of me. But it was not to be. Later, after Louise had been retired for some time and felt that she could no longer live alone in her home in Winchester Center, she came to live for a while in a room on the 3d floor of our Hartford, Connecticut home. True to her own standards of privacy and noninterference in the affairs of others, she was so quiet that we were scarcely aware of her presence and she impinged on our lives only when explicitly invited in. I then learned more of her work with the American Committee for the Protection of the Foreign Born. She was driven to this activity by her New England conscience and the conviction that aliens who had lived for many years in our country should not be harassed, or threatened with deportation, because of their political or union activites. I remember that she linked this concern with her commitment to the Hebrew Scriptures and often quoted the biblical dictum, which appears in various contexts, to the effect that there should be one law both for the citizen and for the resident alien. Commenting on the investigations she had undergone from various governmental agencies, she expressed her appreciation for the moral support received from this college when the pressure was on. I believe she had offered to resign, but I am not certain on that point.

It came as something of a surprise when I learned Louise had been one of the translators of Bultmann's *Jesus* (1926) under the English title *Jesus and the Word* (1934). Mistakenly I had thought of her chiefly as an Old Testament historian with a special interest in the literary-historical problems of Ezekiel. Then I learned she was in the process of translating into English some of Karl Barth's writings. This

*Harvey K. McArthur is Professor Emeritus at the Hartford Seminary in Hartford, Connecticut.

translation was published in 1962 as *Theology and the Church: Shorter Writings, 1920–1928*. Strangely enough I never remember our discussing theology per se. But in thinking back I have recaptured the memory of a comment she made to me about myself which implied that I was a liberal of the better sort, but still not quite the right stuff! Alas, I cannot now probe that issue further with her.

When I think of Louise Pettibone Smith I think of her as the embodiment of the best associated with the phrase "New England character." She had a sharp, unclouded conscience; she was fiercely independent and individualistic; she faced life with realism and acceptance; and she was determined to make life significant. In that she succeeded.

Students Remember Miss Smith

Mary Martin MacRae*

Louise Pettibone Smith was a complex person. She came of a staid old New England family, daughter of the owner and publisher of the local newspaper, and she was proud of it. The knowledge she acquired from her father helped her immeasurably in college, she told me. If she had a flaw, it would have to have been a lack of interest in the bright person less fortunate than she.

When I lived with Miss Smith at Number 1 Hallowell House I enjoyed the ease, peace and quiet, and intellectual stimulation which we shared. I was a student of philosophy, or so I thought myself to be, and at that time I was quite fascinated by Kant and the other idealists whose proponent was Flora Isabel McKinnon. Miss Smith was interested in religion in the larger sense, a three-times graduate of Bryn Mawr College, (and don't you forget it!) where she "really learned something." Bryn Mawr was the best the United States had, she said, but alas! not so good as the German universities. Fifteen summers living with a German professor and his family had convinced her. They were real intellectuals; no others could compare.

We had breakfast together each morning in the large kitchen and we talked of the events of the day, which in 1933 were really something to talk about. There was Roosevelt closing the banks and Pres Pen giving each girl a letter of credit to buy what she wanted (she probably didn't need anything) and the turmoil of the great depression all over this country as well as Europe. Since my experiences were limited indeed when compared to those of Miss Smith, she usually had the first and last words. She couldn't quite make up her mind about Roosevelt: his firm hand was much needed, but then he was a Democrat who had been a Republican. Could anyone really trust him?

*Mary Martin MacRae studied in Wellesley's Graduate School in 1932–1933.

Once, in the village, there was a big to-do about the local priest at one of the churches who was alleged to have been arrested for being drunk, of all things. I was on the spot because he was of the same faith as mine. I never knew the gentleman, but somehow Miss Smith looked to me to explain it. My answer was to ask her what her religious preference was, since she had never told me. She said that she always joined the church which had the greatest impact on the community. It would be there that she could do the most good. If she did not agree with them she could work to change them; if she did agree she could help them with whatever they were doing. Autocratic? Perhaps. Or hypocritical as one of my closest friends suggested? Not necessarily.

One day she came in from a shopping trip to Boston. She had found a silversmith who would melt down the dozen sterling teaspoons which had belonged to her grandmother and make from them eleven spoons of the same design but thicker and stronger where the handle joins the bowl. She was absolutely delighted. I was stunned. The depression was on and the cost of the spoons prohibitive. I am sure I said so. Her position was that she wanted to tell the truth about her spoons when she said they belonged to her grandmother, and how else could she do it? "After all," she said, "it is just as well to let people know you didn't get your money in the last war." Pride in family and heritage went a long way with her, which was natural in that day and time.

But not too long after the spoons were done, she came back from a three-day conference at Bryn Mawr quite annoyed with the proceedings. "Here we sat," said she, "contemplating a piece of broken pottery while the world goes to pieces. It is an awful waste of time." That was carrying it too far. I agreed.

I was touched by her confidence in me. When she was going to be away overnight or for several days, she would tell me that I was monarch of all I surveyed in the apartment. Nothing was ever locked. I appreciated that declaration of confidence and saw to it that things were pretty much as she had left them. After all, I had to show her that I was as well reared as was she.

Miss Smith's Achilles heel was children. She loved them although, generally speaking, one would never have known. Since I was young and had turned twenty-one after I arrived at Wellesley, I thought that it was because she had never married and had romanticized about the joys of having kids. Now, I am not so sure. After the war (World War II) she took her sabbatical and went to Greece where she worked as an aide in a children's hospital. She even learned to use the word "okay" which was considered slang (at that time) and she hated slang. She told me later that children responded to the word, and that was good enough for her.

While I was living at Hallowell, Miss Smith purchased what she called a chicken coop in Connecticut, to which she expected to retire. The challenge was great; she had to learn much about architecture and get the renovation work done when she could find the time. I was surprised that she gave up her family home so easily. "Too big," she said. Years later when the chicken coop was done, she invited me to visit her and see it, but the right time never came. My daughter and I did accept her invitation to visit her at Hallowell House once for a week, and she was a most gracious hostess. We saw more of New England during that visit than I had ever seen before or since.

All the while I stayed with her she talked about the joys of rearing children and how well she thought I would handle it. So, when she received the invitation to my wedding, she was delighted. She visited us in North Carolina and at Lincoln University, Pennsylvania and gave full approval of my children. She was as generous and as kind to them as any doting grandmother. My daughter was her favorite until my younger son came along. He was her heart, and she made no effort to hide it. Once when she was visiting us at Lincoln, I had planned an afternoon in which the children would go to play with their friends, and Miss Smith and I would go for a walk. I was trying to convince my younger son of the merits of such an arrangement without much success—he was all of five going on twenty-five, and without one single insecure bone in his body. Suddenly, she couldn't stand it any longer, so she said very firmly, "Mary, this is nonsense; he would be quite acceptable anywhere at any time during daylight hours." Whereupon she strode across the room, took him firmly by the hand and walked out the front door. Wouldn't you know the little rascal looked over his shoulder and winked at me as he crossed the threshold? I could not find my voice to say anything at all. That was just as well. Miss Smith's face had not a trace of repentance on it.

One discussion stands out among the many we had. Hitler was on the rise in Germany doing some horrible things, especially to male youngsters who wouldn't go along with his plans. I was simply stunned, and said so. She was calmer than I. To my dismay she predicted that Hitler would not last long, that the German intellectuals would not tolerate him when they had time to think about it. "Time," I said, "good heavens, people are dying." All of us know the answer to that one, and no one more than I wished I had not won that round. She was not insensitive but was at times willing to let things work out. Always the bright ones at Harvard or Bryn Mawr or Heidelberg would take care of things before they got too bad. I was young and hoped that she would be proven right. But I was also a Negro, and anyone who thinks that isn't an everyday frightening experience ought to try it for a year. Someone once said that eternal vigilance is the price one must pay for democracy, and with that in mind I kept watch through the whole torturesome ordeal. We never discussed it later because it seemed to me that any reference to her earlier position was painful to her.

Later, when I reflected on Kant's moral law, it occurred to me that were it to be followed exactly, we might end up with the same kind of world we have already. Each person has his own idea of what he would like everyone else to do, so that people from different cultures would only underscore the culture they were brought up to accept as the best. I remember thinking that surely Miss Smith had not thought of that because if she had she would have said, "Mary, if you had gone to Bryn Mawr you would have arrived at that conclusion much earlier."

The whole thing offers a tricky balance. I am sure Kant, with his high sounding philosophy and well-chosen words, would have been able to combine it into a reasonable moral law, but at the time, I found it impossible. As a personal philosophy I believe in Kant, but then Kant never traveled more than one hundred miles from his home in Königsberg. Neither he nor anyone else can speak for all the diverse people of the world.

It is hard to believe, but Louise Pettibone Smith was a bit dubious about equal rights for women. One day she said to me that she thought it a mistake for married women to take jobs away from home. They took jobs away from men, and lowered their concept of themselves as the provider. Also, if there were children, the children suffered. "But," she added, "women are out, and I don't think there is any way to get them back in. Too bad."

Louise Pettibone Smith was complex. She was also a good friend, intelligent, sincere, generous, and had a genuine concern for the poor of the world. That is enough to ask of any one person. The highest virtues come in short supply. Some of us get one or two, some get a few more, but none of us gets them all. Miss Smith had far more than her share, and she handled them well. Wellesley's own Katherine Lee Bates said it best in her immortal line: "Confirm thy soul in self-control, thy liberty in law." Miss Smith did that and more.

Alice Elder Leake*

Although my graduation preceded the 1951 Bultmann visit, I was among the students in Louise Pettibone Smith's seminar on the Old Testament. We were all awed by the reputation of her seminar as one barely survivable. Although it was true that Louise Pettibone Smith felt that only an insight new to her deserved an A, her seminar remained a high point of Wellesley for me. For she continued her own research with the same unrelenting devotion expected of her students, and she appeared, to us at least, to have personal knowledge of the origin, history and scribal location of nearly every verse in the Bible. It was the conviction of Biblical History majors that the first communication between Louise Pettibone Smith and God Himself would concern the exegesis of those rare passages still in question.

Convinced as we were that Louise Pettibone Smith spent more than all of her time in the study, exposition and critical explanation of biblical texts, it was something of a shock to learn, in her response to our requests for senior recommendations, that her firm and continuing support of the rights of new Americans had earned her a place among those suspected by the House Un-American Activities Committee. She shared this information, concerned that her name would taint ours, by association. We continued to feel that her signature would rather gild our own, and harbored muffled pride in our professor whose book on the exegesis of Genesis had been considered a subversive document—until a colleague of the examiner kicked him under the trial table.

An early warning signal that one's seminar report was not on course was the describing of circles by her crossed foot, a warning which, when heeded, could save everyone precious time, omitting the offending passage to continue on surer ground. Tea was a welcome pause in the three-hour class, and the opportunity to exchange opinions was always welcome.

The last time we were together in the same room was at an evening lecture by a visiting professor from Chicago. Pettibone Smith had arranged for someone to give me a ride, as I was then on crutches. As

*Alice Elder Leake graduated from Wellesley in 1950.

always, the postlecture question period proved irresistible, until the then-chairman of the department silenced me with, "What does she mean, standing between heaven and earth and asking questions?" I shall always be grateful to Louise Pettibone Smith for coming up to me afterward, not only to answer the offending question, but to say that it was, indeed, for questions that she had been anxious for me to attend.

We do miss her here, but what discussions they must be having up in Heaven! And what gratitude from those for whom she made real the promise of America!

Priscilla Ham Alexander*

As a Biblical History major, I was privileged to take several classes with Louise Pettibone Smith—required Sophomore Bible, Old Testament, Hebrew language, and a Church History seminar. Let me tell you of one incident which solidified my respect for her. At the close of one seminar session in which I had clearly demonstrated that I was not prepared for class, she asked me to stay behind and then inquired as to the reason for my unpreparedness. With fear and trembling I confessed that I had found a copy of *Gone With the Wind* in which I had been engrossed for several days. There was a long pause and then she said very firmly—with a twinkle in her eye, "Go home and finish that book as fast as you can, and then let's get back down to business!" I never again went unprepared to her class.

Miss Smith was truly a great teacher, informed in her field and appreciative of the young women she taught. I shall always be grateful for the role she played in making my Wellesley education such a valuable and enduring experience.

*Priscilla Ham Alexander graduated from Wellesley in 1948.

Pearl Kosby Russo*

Although I had not known Miss Smith personally when I was a Wellesley student, I met her in 1948. At her invitation, my husband, son and I visited her at her summer house in Washington, Connecticut, to express our appreciation for her defense of the foreign born. We came away from the visit with a deep admiration for this tall, handsome woman with a winning smile and gentle personality, but who had strong convictions that this country, for which her ancestors had fought the American Revolution, belonged to all of us. That was my only personal contact with Miss Smith, but I continued to hear of her, several years later, through my sister, who worked with Miss Smith in the American Committee for the Protection of the Foreign Born.

Miss Smith spent much time in Germany, where she studied the Confessing Church and its relation to the Hitler regime. Deeply affected by her experiences in Hitler Germany, she felt impelled, in the following years, to speak out and to act when she saw similar developments in the United States. In December 1951, after the McCarran Internal Security Act had been passed, Miss Smith accepted the co-chairmanship of the American Committee for the Protection of the Foreign Born, a post she filled with distinction for almost three decades.

She was born in Ogdensburg, New York, in 1887, the only daughter of A. A. Smith, editor of the *Ogdensburg Journal* and the *Saint Lawrence County Republican*. In speaking of her youth, she once commented, "Those were the days when the Republican Party was still very much the party that freed the slaves, the party of Lincoln."

At a time when Wellesley students are discussing career versus volunteerism, I think of Louise Pettibone Smith. She did not have to debate the question, for her long life combined both aspects of contributing to society. A member of the Wellesley faculty for thirty-eight years, she exemplifies for me the embodiment of our motto—*Non Ministrari, sed Ministrare.*

*Pearl Kosby Russo graduated from Wellesley in 1932.